SELF-CARE 101

RENÉE!
Yay fellow
bitch-slapper.
Thanks for
celebrating
with me.
01.26.16

SELF-CARE 101

A GUIDE TO NOURISH & FLOURISH TEAM YOU

≫→ SHELLEY HUNTER HILLESHEIM →

BIG FISH PRESS

Denver, CO

Self-Care 101: A Guide to Nourish and Flourish Team YOU
Published by Big Fish Press
Denver, CO

Library of Congress Control Number: 2015956378

Hillesheim, Shelley Hunter, Author
Self-Care 101: A Guide to Nourish and Flourish Team YOU
Shelley Hunter Hillesheim

ISBN: 978-0-9967623-0-4

SELF-HELP/Self-Management

QUANTITY PURCHASES: Schools, companies, professional groups, clubs, and other organizations may qualify for special terms when ordering quantities of this title. For information, email Shelley@ANourishedLife.net.

DEDICATION

To the expanding tribe of self-care and total wellness warriors,
and all who may connect with this book in meaningful,
life-altering ways—this one is for you!

"Each friend represents a world in us, a world not born until they
arrive, and it is only by this meeting that a new world is born."
~Anais Nin

My heartfelt hope is that this material is that new world for you.

I celebrate each and every person that is touched by this work.
I believe we are the new breed of shero.

CONTENTS

Preface – My Self-Care Journey

Introduction – Living Self-Care

MY SELF-CARE JOURNEY

"In the broken places, the light can shine through."
~Leonard Cohen

This book isn't about me. I wrote it for you. However, it seems impossible for me to take you on a personal self-care journey without telling you a little of my own story first.

After a lifetime of choices and experiences, I landed right smack in the middle of what would become the most critical, defining period of my life thus far. You know how it goes . . . from the ashes we rise, but unfortunately that means bottoming out first. Isn't that how it always seems to work? It was no different for me.

I've had many defining moments in my life, but there was something different about this particular period. Life circumstances "crescendoed" in such a way that I was led to the exact point where I needed to be at exactly the moment I needed to be there. Life is sneaky like that. As a result, I have changed and shaped myself more in the past few years than ever before. I guess I was ready for the big lessons.

As I painfully approached finding the bottom of my own tank, I knew I wanted to feel better, and I felt that *perhaps* it was time to get the help I really needed. I was deeply lost and *feeling incredibly sorry for myself.* I felt like I was crumbling into tiny pieces. I had lost the ability to see the big picture and was in a very dark place. I seriously wanted to run away. I am sure I had mentioned how I was feeling a time or two to friends, family, and anyone I felt comfortable enough to share with. At the time, that list was very short, because I was relatively closed off from being vulnerable with other people.

Several times over a period of a few months, I found myself sitting in my vehicle in the garage, crying my eyes out, or pacing the hallway trying to figure out how I was going to announce to my family that I *really* needed a break and wanted to escape. I knew I needed help, but I wasn't entirely sure where to begin.

I wanted people in my life to show up differently for me, to understand my struggles, to see what I needed, and to come to my aid. I was disappointed on a regular basis when no one showed up. I thought I was sharing what was going on with those closest to me. Well, kind of, maybe. However, I could not escape the idea that everyone was so "busy," they did not have time for my crap. Even if someone did *kind of* show up, no one ever showed up *exactly* the way I wished they would. At the time, I thought that maybe I would have had more help if people really, really knew what was going on, or lived closer to me, or had more time, but it felt too exhausting to reach out differently than what I had already tried, which wasn't netting me much.

I knew I needed consistent help, but I did not know where that would come from. I felt terribly alone and isolated, even in a roomful of people. I simmered in my disappointment, wishing that I could write people a script for what they should say and how they could support me.

At that time, I was about ten months into an arrangement that was the catalyst for leading me to this massive state of frustration. My husband had accepted a new job with a company out of state, after being unemployed for two years. He worked and lived in California during the week and came home to Denver on the weekends. It was not an ideal circumstance by any means, but it was an answer to a prayer in so many ways.

My husband's unemployment had created *immense* stresses in our lives. This job, plus the benefits it would provide, felt like a light at the end of the tunnel, which was a major relief considering the grim and stressful circumstances we had been experiencing during his unemployment. He and I had many conversations about how his new position would impact our lives before making the final decision, including talks with our two children, who were eight and ten at that time. We got their input because we knew that things were about to get really different for them as well. We discussed, for maybe a minute, the idea of moving the entire family, but the resistance was too great from all of us. The cost of living would at least quadruple, and we had too much rooted in where we were.

The whole situation of having my husband commute between California and Colorado felt colossal, but we decided as a family that we wanted to give it a go. I *kind of* knew what I was in for, but it is true—we never *really* know what it's going to be like until we "live" a situation. Each of us has our own version of what it looks like when the wheels come off in our lives. For me, this was where the wheels got loose.

After ten months of being a single parent during the week and a very involved co-parent on the weekends, I found myself bordering on a nervous breakdown. During those months, I had navigated various intense issues with the kids as they transitioned to our new way of life, worked diligently to be a successful entrepreneur, nursed significant bodily injuries sustained in my years of being a competitive figure athlete, managed all aspects of running our household, and was the sole decision-maker for my ailing grandmother. I also worked through the stresses of parenting differently when I was alone versus how I parented when my husband was around. My health took a toll, too, as I suffered with multiple physical issues, including lifelong chronic migraines that were now at a pace of twenty days per month, and experienced daily debilitating panic/anxiety attacks. I was feeling so overwhelmed with "life" that I couldn't even fathom what it would feel like to actually begin to make my self-care a priority.

I often spent time on the weekends in bed feeling lethargic and depressed. I always felt relieved when my husband got home on the weekends to help with the kids, but then I mostly wanted to escape to have some time alone, which then elicited a deep sense of guilt. One of the things I know deeply about myself is that I require a certain amount of alone time on a regular basis to keep my head above water, and I wasn't getting *any, at all,* for many, many months in a row. My emotions were in hyper-sensitive mode most of the time, fluctuating from one extreme of emotions to another. My threshold for any added stress was extremely low, and my thoughts were constantly scattered. I could barely muster the energy to function on a daily basis. I might have had a few days in a row of manageable "happiness," which on the outside may have seemed like I was doing all right. On the inside, however, I felt trapped and dead, going through the motions but not really living.

On top of everything that had changed at home, I also experienced a random act of violence that left me feeling incredibly violated. Someone broke into my vehicle, demolished it, and stole everything inside, which amounted to thousands of dollars in damage to my vehicle and several more thousand in items stolen. I couldn't help questioning how this had happened. *Why did I leave so many things in my truck?* The life experiences just kept piling on.

My husband was as supportive as he could be while also managing a new job, his own transition to living and working in another state, exercise, frequent travel, and missing his family during the week. The reality was that he was not home. He was not physically present, and I knew I needed more.

One day, after another bout of serious depression, including several days in bed, I managed to muster enough clarity to realize that I needed a new way to take care of myself and that the real hero of my story *had to be* me. I couldn't wait for others to come to my rescue and save me. I couldn't expect them to show up in a certain way and fix me. This realization was the gift of awakening that I didn't know was coming. I'm not sure why then, why at that particular moment, but my entire life began a shift that changed everything from that moment on.

It was time to give up my victim card and take action. I had to do something because I was completely exhausted with the way things were. So, at that moment, feeling completely broken, I made a powerful *choice* to begin what would become an incredibly life-changing and deeply healing self-care journey. I knew deep down that I was the *only* one who could do this work. I couldn't rely on anyone else to do it for me. I also recognized that a powerful part of my story was in landing and sitting in the broken place, checking in on where I was and getting in touch with who I wanted to be instead.

I announced to my family that things were about to get real, and I haven't looked back since. First, I hired a life coach "slash" therapist to begin to help me unravel the mess. I searched high and low for a life coach who I connected with, and who took insurance, which I discovered is a rare find. Once I found her, I had no idea what I was really in for. I recall proclaiming in my initial visit that I had no intention of delving into my past. I had read hundreds of self-help books over the years and had recently researched the idea of life coaching versus therapy, so I was feeling a little self-righteous. I was much more interested in the life coaching approach where we would talk about what is relevant right now in order to move forward. I did not want to spend time swimming around in my childhood, analyzing why I am the way I am. She heard me, I thought, and we were set to go.

I had done therapeutic work in the past to help me navigate through some grueling circumstances, but this felt different. It was more profound on so many levels. It was work with a capital "W." It felt different because it was such a conscious choice to seek out and do this work. It was so important to me, in fact, that I interviewed a half-dozen potential life coaches to find the right one. I was ready to dig in and do more than cope through the circumstances, like I had experienced in therapy in years past. This work included loads of challenging discussions, oceans of seemingly uncontrollable tears, thoughtful reflection, courageous conversations with people in my life, and homework (yes, there is homework in therapy). As you might guess, we delved into my past—*way* into it. Her theory was that I needed to address those sensitive pieces of my past in order to heal those layers and be able to step into the present.

We tackled massive life-altering concepts that led to tremendous healing. We carefully tapped into the most tender parts of my past and were able to uncover some significantly eye-opening concepts, which included:

√ no longer viewing myself as *broken;*

√ letting go of my fear of abandonment (still
  a work in progress, by the way, because
  it shows up everywhere for me);

√ releasing feeling sorry for a missed childhood
  due to family circumstances;

√ resurfacing and tackling suppressed garbage from
  a gruelingly painful and very personal medical
  malpractice lawsuit that took five actual years
  of my life and still affects me to this day;

√ coping with my father's suicide right after I got
  married and, by default, taking on the responsibility of
  making all decisions around my grandmother's care;

√ navigating sensitive issues regarding my
  relationship with my mother

√ acknowledging anger and loads of resentment; and

√ boldly facing my type-A-perfectionist side that is
  incessantly trying to prove my worth, as well as
  constantly being in warrior/survivor mode.

We also tackled a *lot* of other critical things, such as
understanding what I need at any particular moment and learning
to ask for it, taking responsibility for the way I feel, letting myself
feel without judging it, gently releasing that which no longer serves
me, creating a much-needed support system, and finding ways to
love myself through the healing. To aid in my journey, I also tapped
into other powerful resources like self-development books, classes,

workshops, and reconnected with my spirituality in new ways. I was all in, and it felt pretty much like a full-time job.

Slowly, but surely, over the course of a year, the muddy waters started to settle. I was beginning to see the bottom of the lake through the muck. I navigated my way through the darkness, not just looking at what was happening at that time but considering my whole life. In time, I was catapulted into a new era of transformative self-care practices that changed my entire being. I built Team ME in this process by crafting an entire support structure around what I needed, not in a selfish way, but in a very self-nourishing way.

Giving myself permission and allowing myself to make the space to connect with the wisdom that my struggles provided was the most precious gift I have ever given myself. I was able to release the paralyzing panic and anxiety, have real conversations without the fear of being judged, build a meaningful support system, including a sisterhood of amazing women, and ultimately create structure and sacred discipline around foundational self-care practices that allow me to show up as ME.

I learned how to live unapologetically, to focus on really being present and making real connections in my life. I have changed so much in the last few years that I barely recognize who I was before. That is a priceless gift. I climbed out of a victim mentality into my power and fell in love with myself again. I began the tremendous process of finding my truth and knowing what to do to re-connect with it at times when I notice that it has fuzzier edges than I desire. I no longer spend much time in a warrior, survivor, self-protection mode, which is baffling, given my lifetime of protecting myself from pain and fear. I was able to uncover my vulnerability and get real with myself about what I truly needed in order to find peace and ultimately joy. This awareness has brought a whole new sense of grace into my life. I am still a work in progress, as we all are, but it's with an entirely new awareness.

I allow myself to remain open to the many teachers around me in everyday life, especially my own children. I am committed to a life where I continue to grow, nurture, and learn more about myself and how to better connect with the world of awesomeness around me.

I originally launched my brand, A Nourished Life, after completing my Nutritional Chef education, to teach people how to take ownership of their nutrition by making conscious food choices and through re-introducing them to their kitchens by teaching them basic cooking techniques. At the time, I truly thought that would save the world, and maybe it did in some small way. However, as my experience in working with people evolved, I recognized that there was so much more to self-care than just what we put in our mouths. I had been doing forms of "coaching" in the way I approached my nutrition and cooking programs, but I longed for a more structured way to be a brighter light for other women in addressing all aspects of self-care as a foundation to total wellness. I wanted to figure out a way to combine my own self-care journey with my desire to expand my business service offerings.

I am proudly addicted to school, so in addition to a Bachelors in Science in Marketing, an MBA, tax preparation and securities licensing, as well as a Nutritional Chef certification, I went back to school to learn more about how to help people experience sustainable transformation. This time it was health and lifestyle coaching. And this time, I found my passion and purpose!

While I recognize that everyone must live their own journey, if there is a way to help other women hand over the victim card and step into owning their self-care needs sooner, I want to offer my support. Part of my passion and purpose is to help other ambitious women create meaningful self-care practices for their own busy lives so they can experience true vitality without shame or guilt. This book is the culmination of everything I have personally experienced, formally studied about self-care, and come to know about how to live it like you mean it.

INTRODUCTION
LIVING SELF-CARE

I'm not a PhD or a researcher, and I am likely not the profound philosopher I'd like to think I am at times. However, I have studied the ideas of self-care, nourishment, and transformation extensively and formally for many years. And I continue to pursue new knowledge almost daily. I am in constant learning mode, and I wouldn't have it any other way. It's a huge part of how I nourish and flourish. I have gained tremendous perspective over the years on new ways of thinking, doing, and being that can help create transformation. I know that everything I've read and experienced has been a fundamental part of my own journey to land me where I am at this moment, where I can embody a life steeped in self-care and renewal. As a result, I have built an incredibly supportive Team ME and feel honored to be able to share all of these insights with you.

While I've read loads of personal development books, the element that always seems to be missing is HOW TO implement new ways of thinking, and this has always frustrated me. I often read about and get inspired by a new concept for living my life in a more connected way, but much of the time, the author doesn't tell me *how* to do it. Many of the books I've read shed light on how our current way of *being* isn't serving us. Most of the time the solutions offered are centered around the idea that in order to feel better you have to change the way you think. I definitely agree with that. Changing the way we think is powerful, but I've honestly never been able to just say to myself, "Start thinking differently," and then go. I always want to learn more about *how* I actually get from where I am now to where I want to be. *How* do I actually bridge that gap? My assumption is that others feel the same way, so this book is a powerful nod to the HOW!

Because of what I've experienced and been frustrated by, I want to not only share philosophies around ways of thinking, doing, and being, but to give you tools to actually make the changes. *Self-Care 101* is my idea of a "how to" anthem. It contains loads of how-tos and ample tools so that you can take powerful, meaningful, and inspired action steps based on your most fundamental needs. It's a guide for *how to* make self-care a priority in an already hectic life. It will also fundamentally help you identify your vision and your *why* for wanting to dive deeper into a self-care centered way of living, so you can connect with the total impact of giving yourself this gift, which means you get to experience the vast benefits of tending to your self-care needs in mind, body, and soul. This total impact includes your now, your future, and every other person you interact with in your life.

While there are endless ways you can address self-care, in this book, we will be focusing on the big three—mind, body, and soul—along with the key activities you can do within each area to help nourish and flourish Team YOU. Team YOU is the idea that we each have the power to create the support system we need, our own personal wellbeing team, so to speak. While the work begins with us, many, many others in our lives play a critical role. Team YOU recognizes the team effort. If you can create a systematic rhythm of healthy self-care habits around each one of the three primary areas, along with a support system to ensure your success, you are practically guaranteed a more complete and fulfilled life where you can be present and actually feel joy in your day-to-day living.

Self-care is a continuous commitment to the fundamental needs that center a person's entire being. *Self-Care 101* will provide you with tools to help you navigate the mental and physical nature of inspired self-care living along with the tangible how-tos to create your desired self-care experience, make powerful choices, and transform your circumstances. You probably already recognize the profound need for self-care in your life, which is a big piece of why you've picked up this book. Once you find your self-care happy place, it is truly a beautiful synergy of mind, body, and soul.

Living a life steeped in self-care is so much more than simply being conscious of how you treat yourself. And it's far more than pampering yourself or being taken care of. Living a life centered around self-care is your biggest ally. It not only deeply nourishes you but also nourishes every single other person that is impacted by your presence in this lifetime. Truly profound, don't you think? It's taking care of yourself in meaningful, fulfilling, energy-renewing ways, and when you are really doing the work, it becomes a compass for how you express yourself and how you feel about yourself. Imagine waking up every day feeling refreshed, loved, and supported. Imagine knowing exactly what needs to get done in order to fulfill your passion and purpose. A dream? It can become a reality as you begin to focus on tending to regular self-care practices, which will then allow you to live and think more mindfully.

Seeing yourself as the beautiful epicenter of an amazing lifetime experience where you can honor and cherish your body, mind, and soul is sacred work. It's a way of *being* in the world. It's not an action item on a to-do list or a pursuit where you arrive at an end goal. It's your essence and your way of moving through your life. It's the entire way you sense your own worthiness and act out your life from that centered, grounded place steeped in self-care and self-love. As you learn more about what self-care is and the ways in which you can better nourish and flourish, you will unleash a new flow about your life that creates more space to experience yourself and your life in a more purposeful and intentional way.

We'll be exploring many ways to build your own sacred self-care practices. I call what you will create "practice" because it's an ever-renewing process. You don't simply set your intentions by creating a course of action that you plan to carry out in some way and then forget about. You live those intentions and practice them each and every day. To make self-care a way of life requires a "habit review" to identify where you are selling yourself short and where you can make upgrades. It's disrupting the energies and patterns of old, tired stories and releasing them so you can construct more nurturing stories and ways of being.

In most cases, the tools you will use throughout this book are in the form of an exercise or a Self-Care Dare, my challenge to you to put what you read into practice. I also provide downloadable forms to assist you in that process. I promise that I've kept the workload manageable. The idea is not to overwhelm you. However, using the tools is essential for you to get the most out of the material. The real magic, the sweet spot in nourishing and flourishing Team YOU, is in doing the work and taking continuous inspired actions. The principles, philosophies, exercises, and dares throughout this book will help you break the habit of old conditioning and step into new, more empowered awareness.

We are responsible for our own life story, and that responsibility takes root when we decide to take charge of that story, no longer blaming, projecting, or depending on someone else. If you give away that responsibility, it also gives away the control that must be owned by you alone. Taking control also gives you the rights to the joy and bliss of your story. It takes time for this to become your personal reality, so this book is a guide to hold your hand through the journey and arrive at new practices that honor self-care as your center, which will propel you to do what you are *really here* to do in this life.

The process that will unfold for you throughout this book is a simple framework for sustainable self-care success. It takes into account human decision-making, motivation, and behavior, moving you beyond the excuse of hectic schedules and the "too busy" mindset. We will be creating changes that are relevant to you and your life, setting you up to get fully engaged in living. To honor that effort, we will look at self-care and self-nurturing, without you white knuckling and willpower-ing your way through. We will not be force-feeding any circumstances that do not serve you. It's about connecting with who you really are and where you are by first taking the time to sit with yourself in order to clear out the space and figure out your true self-care needs. From there you can re-establish your beliefs about what counts.

Our journey together will begin in Part One by clearly defining what self-care is and what it isn't, in an effort to expand your awareness and potentially dispel some old myths. We also explore the current state of self-care in a broad sense, define ideal self-care, and then tap into an assessment tool that will give you a much clearer sense of where you are in your current self-care practices. Additionally, we begin some bite-sized self-care dares at the end of each chapter to keep you engaged in the self-care development process as you move through the book. Don't skip these. They offer you time for reflection and self-understanding, which all build towards something big in the final chapters of the book.

We then move on to Part Two, where we uncover the most important question you can ask yourself when beginning any transformation, then move on to principles that focus on ways to honor yourself, such as the art of choosing yourself as a priority and the power of setting boundaries that serve you well. We also touch on the importance of clearing out and making space for work on self-care.

Part Three focuses entirely on ways to nourish your beautiful body, including ways to love it differently; inspiration for addressing nagging ailments; ways to feed it, including mindful consumption techniques along with fabulous meal planning tools. Additionally, we will cover new ways of thinking to move that body to support physical activity while also focusing some emphasis on the power of having play in your life and getting proper rest.

In Part Four we embark upon the myriad of ways to nourish your mind and soul with an emphasis on purposeful pause and the mother of all ways to connect with your inner wisdom—meditation. We will cover the importance of downtime and stillness, and spend some time on the importance of gratitude, connection, creative expression, community, and being of service to others, in your life and your work.

Part Five highlights the ways to set yourself up for inevitable success, removing any barriers so that you can almost guarantee your success with making self-care a new priority in your life. In this section, we also look at intentions and goals, along with support, accountability, and the extreme power you have over your time when you begin your day in a certain way.

In the final section, Part Six, we reveal new ways to think about how to evaluate your particular journey. We end with an exercise that ties everything together to serve as a visual mantra and compass for your new self-care empowerment journey to nourish and flourish Team YOU, which is the compilation of not only your own beliefs and subsequent supporting actions, but resources of people, places, and things that will help you maintain a life dedicated to self-care.

The highest purpose of this book is to help you connect with and form independent thoughts about what you need and what will work for you in building your team around your most fundamental self-care needs. The key is to step out of what is no longer serving the needs of your mind, body, and soul and begin to develop your own path for going forward. Believe it or not, the process of finding what works and discovering your own self-care path gives your life new meaning. It sanctifies your purpose and passion in new and profound ways, and it can become your greatest legacy.

My intention is that you will use this book as your guide to create awareness around the power and purpose of self-care and to build a plan that can be your working foundation. This will anchor you into a peaceful way of living during times that seem to flow easily and also be a springboard out of the abyss when life gets messy. It can also serve as a go-to tool to help you stay the course and hold yourself to higher self-care standards no matter what is going on around you.

It is my absolute honor to share this with you. It is my passionate desire to help you live a life filled to the brim with self-care practices that nourish your body, mind, and soul. I want to illuminate a path for you that may feel like a stretch, but I promise that if you stay the course, it will ultimately settle into a natural way of existence as you grow with the flow.

The following are the tools you will need as you read this book and complete the exercises:

- ☑ An open mind and heart.
- ☑ A small journal (I suggest that you label it "Self-Care Journal"). Find a journal you love and keep it with this book so you can do the exercises as you go.
- ☑ Your favorite writing instrument.

As we embark on this journey together, I want to express to you how powerful this process can be. For that reason, I feel deeply called to share the knowledge that I have collected from years of reading, researching, self-help, therapy, workshops, education, my own personal journey, and working with many clients. The concepts I share here are the self-care success equation I have developed for myself and in my coaching practice. I am not presenting a quick fix system. It's a framework—a way to think about and set yourself up for "inevitable success" in your daily self-care habits, along with ideas for reflection that activate your connection with what you do day in and day out to support your self-care needs. It's real life, it's practical, and it's my gift to you!

part 1

<< — WHAT IS SELF-CARE? — >>

"Love yourself first, and everything else falls in line. You really have to love yourself to get anything done in this world."
~ Lucille Ball

CHAPTER ONE
←— FOUNDATIONS —→

The most important relationship you have in this life is the one you have with yourself. Period. Honoring that relationship is the basic essence of self-care. Self-care isn't just about the ways we honor our bodies by addressing nutrition and calories, although those are powerful components. Self-care includes all aspects of how we nourish our bodies, minds, and souls. It's the whole YOU package that honors and nurtures your fundamental needs, far beyond your pressing list of "shoulds." Standing in and owning your self-care needs nourishes your entire life, who you are, and how you want to live.

Quite simply, we cannot give to anyone what we do not have within ourselves. By giving yourself more, you are able to give more. It's like when you are on a plane before takeoff and the flight attendants give instructions for what to do if there is a decrease in cabin air pressure. Passengers are instructed to put on their own oxygen mask first, *before* assisting anyone else. Self-care is your oxygen mask. Once you know how to place it properly, it will stay in place for the rest of your life. It's the act of filling your cup first and then offering to others from the overflow. I guarantee that if you truly fill your cup first, there will be overflow. If your cup isn't full, you cannot truly show up for any other activity or any other person in your life. You end up settling for only a small portion of yourself, even when you might fundamentally know there is so much more potential.

Self-care is a major piece of the foundation of your life, as important as air, water, breathing, food, and shelter. Despite what you might be thinking, self-care is not the same thing as pampering, although some pampering is certainly nice every now and then. At its root, self-care includes any *intentional* actions you take to care for your physical, mental, emotional, and spiritual wellbeing. All of those aspects are absolutely integrated. It's buying time for yourself and making yourself a priority, not in a superficial way, but in a way that sets you up to show up more fully in every other area of your life. When you do that, it creates a ripple effect of goodness for every single person that is impacted by your presence. What could be more important than that?

While it might not seem immediately obvious, at the heart of self-care is the idea of self-love, which is the over-arching theme that supports the concepts of self-compassion, self-worth, self-kindness, and any other thought or belief you have about your own value and needs. In fact, some researchers suggest that underneath virtually all suffering lies a lack of self-love. If that's true, and I believe it is, we can have so much more control over what we experience in life by learning to *love ourselves up*. Sounds simple, but I know how monumentally challenging it can be for many of us. The other profound piece of the self-love principle is that our entire capacity to truly love and celebrate any other person in our lives is directly connected to our ability to fully love ourselves first. It makes sense then that we first need to take a deeper look at self-love as a powerful part of the self-care process.

In case the need for self-love isn't immediately obvious to you, here are a few signs that that part of YOU needs some loving attention.

- ✔ You are quick to criticize yourself.
- ✔ You don't take care of your body the way you'd like because "other things" are more important.
- ✔ You place other people's needs above your own so often that you are worn down and depleted.
- ✔ You spend sleepless nights replaying dramas that you wish you'd handled differently, inwardly beating yourself up over them.
- ✔ You tend to make your emotional pain worse by turning to addictions as a way to soothe.
- ✔ You seem to have a lot of crises in your life.
- ✔ Your inner voice has a way of speaking to you in a negative way.

Do you resonate with any of these circumstances? Essentially, our self-love, and ultimately the way we care for ourselves in general, is reflected in our behaviors and ways of being, such as the quality of our running inner dialogue, how we approach life, with whom we choose to spend time, the image we project, and how we approach challenging circumstances. Self-love teaches us to see all of this with new awareness. After all, we are the sages of our soft spots and our edges—those areas beyond the limits of our comfort zone.

Self-love and self-care is showing up for ourselves with honesty, telling ourselves the truth with love and kindness, and having a willingness to see things differently. Self-love offers us the opportunity to tap into all levels of forgiveness. Self-love means not having to be right all the time. It means letting yourself off the hook if you've tried your best and things didn't turn out exactly as planned. You don't have to be better or stronger than anyone else and you get to be the perfectly "imperfect" version of you at all times.

By focusing some intentional energy on the process of self-love and self-care, we get to experience life in a new and refreshing way. As part of that journey, we get to experience the following:

- Let down our guard.
- Accept imperfection as a human condition.
- Stay neutral in our reflections and avoid harsh judgments (of ourselves and others).
- View life with training wheels attached (meaning we view it all as an experiment).
- Commit to our own evolution.
- Honor our own personal development process.

Throughout *Self-Care 101*, you will have the opportunity to step into self-care in new ways, which are all forms of self-love. This may mean that you need to create a new awareness and tap into new levels of forgiveness. With *Self-Care 101,* your real self-care journey begins now! Say YES to yourself and keep an open and curious mind throughout this journey. Commit to practicing self-love moment by moment.

↩ SELF-CARE DARE ↩
TAME YOUR INNER DIALOGUE

Let's bring some awareness to your inner dialogue. How do you talk to yourself throughout the day? What tone of voice do you use? What words or phrases do you use? When do you say these things? First, notice these things to become more aware of your inner dialogue. Then, write down in your self-care journal at least five examples of things you say to yourself regularly, and whether you see them as positive or negative. How does it make you feel to review this list?

CHAPTER TWO
←— THE CURRENT STATE OF SELF-CARE —→

You don't have to look too hard to find statistics about where we are with general self-care standards as a culture. We read about, hear about, and experience the lack of self-care in our own lives on a regular basis. As a society, we are stressed out and in a constant state of chronic inflammation in our bodies, which leads to disease, unhappiness, and settling for a life that isn't by design. We are in constant overload, coming from every direction in our lives. Too much to do at work and too much to do at home creates immense stresses and leads to finding our edges with our ability to cope. We lose quality and hours of sleep, move our bodies less, and generally feel overwhelmed. Life is "busy," and literally everything else comes before our own self-care needs.

Some of us have children, and they need to come first. Others of us care for family members in various capacities, and they also must come first. Jobs, relationship circumstances, living situations, children, travel, money, and health concerns take over, and we lose our ability to identify what we really need. Even when we want to try to be more mindful of conscious self-care habits, like eating more nutritionally, there is so much information overload in the marketplace, with much of it being contradictory, that we don't even know where to start.

We might have great intentions and kick off a new healthy habit, to find that the flame of inspiration only lasts a few short days or weeks, without any real transformation. Or we know we need to take care of a nagging health ailment, because our body is sending us a distress signal that we can no longer ignore, so we go to the doctor to get it checked out. We end up walking away with a handful of prescriptions, adding to the confusion and potentially not really addressing the underlying root cause of the condition. More often than not, we are not gaining any insights about how we can really make lifestyle shifts that will create significant change. We end up staying in robot mode, just trying to get by without fully engaging in what life could be, feeling "too busy" and confused to take any action.

Most people's first line of defense when they are suffering with physical ailments is to seek the help of a doctor, not necessarily to look inward and say to themselves, "What can I do differently in my day-to-day living that could positively influence how my body is feeling?" We are confused about how to start that process.

I saw this firsthand when I worked with a doctor's office for a summer while I was completing my health and lifestyle coaching training. The office brought me in to observe patient appointments and offer consultative services for them after they had their appointment with the doctor. In a few minutes of consultative time together, I would try to get a patient set up for success with the protocols the doctor recommended and let them know about my additional coaching services in case they needed more support. More often than not, because my coaching services were an additional cost not covered by insurance, the patients would sit with me in the brief consultation at the doctor's office, but not take it any further. They would not participate in additional coaching support. It broke my heart, because I truly believed that most of them would benefit from additional support in order to actually implement the lifestyle changes recommended by the doctor.

This particular doctor was integrative in his approach to treating his patients. He looked at traditional medical solutions but also discussed lifestyle factors and supplements that could be helpful, always preferring to prescribe supplements and a healthy dose of "lifestyle medicine." However, due to what I perceive to be the constraints of practicing medicine in an insurance-based practice, there was very little additional "free" support available to help them actually *be* successful with the prescribed *lifestyle* shifts.

The reality was that the doctor typically had less than fifteen minutes to spend with each patient, so appointments were brief and did not allow much time to cover detailed questions. Although he did have additional "paid" support services available, many patients were in a hurry and simply wanted something that was easy and "free" to start with. If they had to choose fiscal priorities, which was the case with most patients I saw, they would choose the supplement program first. It was definitely easier to implement, rather than having to take on a regimen that would include more intense work around real lifestyle changes and the need to address things like food, movement, sleep, stress reduction, and more conscious living.

For instance, some patients were told that they should not consume gluten and were handed a two-page document in order to help them navigate those changes. For most people, going off gluten is a monumental task. Most of the patients I worked with didn't even know what gluten was or how pervasive it is. They simply never had to deal with it before. I didn't have the opportunity to see many follow-up patients, but I suspect that most of them didn't actually have success going off gluten by using that two-page handout. Truly going gluten-free takes a solid amount of diligence, research, and tremendous support. Typically, a person has to be highly motivated to do so.

Aside from that, my experience there led me to believe that many of the people coming through that doctor's doors were unaware of the massive impact they could have on their own wellness by making significant positive changes to their day-to-day living choices. Without that awareness, it was far more natural to see and depend on pharmaceutical and supplement-based protocols as the only way. However, I did get to work with a handful of patients who were truly interested in healthy transformation and were eager to do the work. They were exhausted with the way they felt, were ready for real, lasting change, and knew they needed more support to make that happen. In short, they were truly ready for a deeper conversation about lifestyle changes and were able to make significant improvements in their wellbeing and life as a result of that readiness.

My experience with my coaching work thus far has led me to

the conclusion that even if at some point in our lives we were more conscious about what we really needed to feel fulfilled in our self-care needs, somewhere along the way, "life" got in the way and we forgot to be intentional about taking care of ourselves. Sadly, some of us don't even feel like we actually are worth the effort. The truth is that the lack of self-care can be a slow process of self-destruction you might not even recognize until you bottom out. It is a foundational need in all of our lives, and we each experience it in our own individual way.

Unfortunately, most of my clients come to me when they are already at their wits' ends and are just looking for something, anything, to help them sleep better, have more energy, be in a better mood, take off a few excess pounds, and find more time in their lives to actually take care of themselves without feeling guilty. So, the beginning point is always uncovering the layers to find out what's really going on and help them reconnect with what they really want to experience in their lives.

⤮ SELF-CARE DARE ⤮
OBSTACLES TO SELF-CARE

In your self-care journal, list as many obstacles as you can think of that prevent you from taking care of yourself. What gets in the way of taking action on your fundamental self-care needs? Is it time constraints, family obligations, workload, or maybe even simply a lack of desire to do so? Spell it out in detail. Consider what obstacles show up at various times of the day. Is the morning too rushed, or are you too exhausted in the evening? Be specific.

CHAPTER THREE

←— IDEAL SELF CARE —→

Before we dive into getting clarity on what ideal self-care practices might look like, let's first talk about what happens when we neglect ourselves by not tending to our lives with love, care, compassion, and self-care. As harsh as this might sound, neglecting yourself is like saying that nothing else really matters. When you don't take care of what you need the most, you put an invisible filter on and see the world in a completely different light. A light that doesn't serve you well. You may get cranky, depressed, be too sensitive, lack perspective, make snap judgments, have nagging body ailments, lack the ability to sleep, be energy depleted, feel anxious or stressed, feel like you are in total overwhelm, lack joy, lack passion and purpose, suffer in your relationships, not thrive at work, and more. You may simply be coping as best you can while your depleted body and mind begin to break down.

Living under these conditions can eventually become debilitating and start to look like dysfunction. As a result, you may begin to play the resilience card, seeking out quick fixes, perhaps convincing yourself that you are okay. You may label circumstances in a category filed under "deal with it later," which accumulates and eventually backfires. Worse yet, you know you aren't really taking care of yourself, yet you project that you've got it all together. That was me … for years. I still go to some of these places when I am not caring for myself the way I know I need.

Know this—the cornerstone of self-care habits is steeped in the fundamentals we'll be covering. If you neglect any one of these mega-fundamentals for any serious length of time, you will not thrive. It's that simple. Even more important for us women is that our inner light can become dull, which dampens our glow. Picture yourself lounging in your pajamas all day with your greasy hair in a messy bun, moping around because you don't feel right. Not that there aren't times when we need to be in our jammies all day, but this is something different. This is about staying true to your fullest potential.

The point here is you don't want to wait until you hit the bottom to begin this process. Start now. Learn about what you need the most and get re-connected with the healthy, self-loving, and nurturing habits that you want to create. Make a promise to embrace the information in this book so you can live differently, nourishing yourself and your life from the inside out and beginning a process to replenish as often as you need to thrive.

Being committed to self-care is simply practicing habits that support your self-care needs on a regular basis. Having a daily routine is ideal. This string of healthy habits then add up to significant health and lifestyle improvements over time. That is where transformation lives. It's a harmonic and rhythmic flow that continuously honors your needs now and as they change. It's a simple concept, but as we all know, it's not so simple to implement and sustain.

There is no ideal self-care formula I could construct that would meet every person's needs. Each of us comes from a different set of experiences and circumstances; thus, our individual needs are vastly different. That's the beauty of the structure we will be exploring together. Your self-care habits and system will be built on your exact needs. This journey is absolutely yours to own. Keeping that in mind, I would like to first present a basic framework to consider as we navigate this together.

The most profound way to understand the entire idea of self-care that I've seen to date was presented to me when I was in health and lifestyle coaching school. This perspective shifted so much for me that I now regularly use this framework in my own coaching practice. It's the concept of viewing your ultimate nourishment by focusing on both primary and secondary foods.

Primary Foods are the types of nourishment you get in your life that do not include what is actually on your plate. Primary foods fuel your life through engaging in activities like healthy relationships, regular physical activity, having a fulfilling career and a spiritual practice. The idea is that when primary food is in sync with your life rhythms, your life actually feeds you, making what you *actually* eat secondary. Think of primary foods as the activities in life that energize you without any effort. Time flies and you don't pay attention to or even care about the clock. I have also heard this referred to as carefree timelessness. In the book entitled *Integrative Nutrition*, Joshua Rosenthal states, "Sometimes we are fed not by food but by the energy of our lives. These moments and feelings demonstrate that everything is food. We take in thousands of experiences of life that can fulfill us physically, mentally, emotionally and spiritually. We hunger for play, fun, touch, romance, intimacy, love, achievement, success, art, music, self-expression, leadership, excitement, adventure and spirituality. All of these elements are essential forms of nourishment. The extent to which we are able to incorporate them determines how enjoyable and worthwhile our lives feel."

Secondary Foods then are the *actual* foods you choose to consume and with which you nourish your body. It is the real food substances on your plate, as well every single thing that you put into your mouth.

The distinction between primary and secondary foods is important because when you feel less than awesome about your body, you might first seek solutions in the secondary food category. Maybe you aren't happy with the way your body looks and you want to eat better to see physical changes, or you've been told by a doctor that you should eat differently. So, your focus becomes only on eating a certain way to create a desired result, without giving a lot of thought to your own *primary* foods and how to nourish yourself from that vantage point as well.

Additionally, on the flip side, you can be on target with your *secondary* foods, doing a bang-up job of eating a perfectly balanced plate and being incredibly mindful of everything you put into your mouth, but you may still not be seeing the expected results. I've certainly been there a time or ten. The problem is that you are only addressing one of the major factors in the total self-care puzzle. The secret is striking a balance with both primary and secondary foods in your life, which is what we will focus on to help you shape that experience.

It's important to remain kind to yourself and recognize that the balance between primary and secondary foods will continue to shift as your needs change. Being in the flow of knowing what you need at any given time is also a must. It keeps you in tune with your ever-changing needs so you can always be in a place to honor those needs depending on your circumstances.

The concept of primary and secondary foods really showed up in my life when I was still teaching nutritionally-centered cooking classes, but I didn't yet have a label for what I was experiencing. I came out of my natural food chef culinary program believing with my entire being that if everyone learned to cook more at home and was mindful of the quality of food they consumed, their entire lives would transform into a mecca of happiness. They'd feel better, have more energy, and be more satisfied in life. I also believed that regular physical activity was important, but I saw the idea of what we put in our mouths as the single most important factor for physical change. Have you ever heard of the saying that abs are made in the kitchen, not in the gym? I believed in that concept wholeheartedly. In fact, I built my entire initial business model within this belief system and passionately pursued the idea to re-introduce people to their kitchens, to get comfy there and learn to care about what they consumed.

At the time, I was still teaching hands-on, healthy-themed cooking classes under a recreational cooking structure at a couple of cooking schools in my area. The classes were three hours long.

During each class, I guided the students through cooking an entire five-course meal. We ended class by eating what they had prepared family style. It was incredibly rewarding work. Based on the feedback I received, I know it definitely helped people see that healthy cooking and eating can be delicious and fun.

Within a couple of years, it became apparent that one three-hour class with me, or even several three-hour classes, could only provide so much help for people to create real and lasting wellness changes. As a result, I began to develop programs for people where I went into their homes and worked with them for eight sessions over eight weeks in a very structured way, taking them on a journey to learn about real foods, kitchen equipment, knife skills, complete pantry purges, meal planning, and basic cooking instruction. In essence, I taught them a mini-version of what I'd learned in my nutritional chef training program. The people who hired me were typically looking to cook and eat better to solve their health problems, get more energy, or feel better in their bodies. Working closely with people in their own home environments, I got to see, hear, and connect with what was really going on for them. I got an insider view of their most intimate home life circumstances, and it gave me an entirely new awareness. I learned that I could get them all set up for cooking and healthy-eating success, and I could teach them how to prepare and eat all of the broccoli and kale in the world. However, if they were struggling in other areas of their lives—such as relationships, sleep, career, spirituality, stress management, or inactivity—my program barely scratched the surface of actual transformation. It absolutely helped, but it became crystal clear to me that there was so much more to the self-care puzzle than simply what we put in our mouths. I only worked with a handful of clients in this capacity before my eyes were wide open. That's when I enrolled in a health and lifestyle coaching program to learn more about how to help people truly transform and get them into action as quickly as possible.

Based on my work with women and my own personal experiences in tending to self-care as a priority, there are many ways life can take new shape as a result, and they are all dependent upon what matters most to us. As I've collected stories regarding shifts into a more self-care focused and self-loving way of being, the most impactful benefit I've discovered is the achievement of a deep sense of inner peace—truly knowing that all is well, always. It's also knowing that even if life doesn't feel like it in the moment at hand, it will be well . . . because we have all of the tools we need to easily get ourselves back to center and back to what matters. This allows us to live this life with more wholeness, to get back to our sacred center as often as possible and begin again, to be energetic, joyful, and happy, while playing bigger, being courageous, and basically being an all-around badass.

∾ SELF-CARE DARE ∾
YOUR IDEAL SELF-CARE VISION

Before we move forward, let's take a moment for you to consider your ideal self-care vision. This is your opportunity to dream a little. I like to think of this as your "possible life," where you can begin to imagine what it could be like if there were no obstacles in the way of living a life dedicated to self-care and self-love.

In your self-care journal, describe *in detail* what your life would be like if you were able to tend to all of your self-care needs. Consider what activities you would participate in, who would be there, how you'd feel on a daily basis, what you would do differently than you do now, and what you would do that you weren't able to do before. Paint a vivid picture in your mind and write down your thoughts. Then, reflect on how you would feel to be able to live like that.

CHAPTER FOUR

« WHERE ARE YOU? »

THE CIRCLE OF SELF-CARE

Your ideal starting point is right where you are. Nothing more, nothing less. All you need to begin is a desire to create a different experience in your life. Chances are you are looking for inspiration and how-to ideas for creating more self-care goodness in your own life. I have designed a self-care assessment tool based on another tool called the Wheel of Life, which is used by many life coaches. My *Circle of Self-Care* tool is extremely useful in bringing a new awareness to where you are right now. I use it in the very first meetings with new coaching clients. It gives me a great idea of where we can prioritize our efforts, and it's an eye-opener for people, showing them an overview of where imbalances might exist. This then provides great insight as to what might need first priority in lifestyle shifts. The best part is that each of these areas can be addressed with specific self-care practices.

I invite you to try out this tool for yourself to see where you are in this moment. You can do it right in this book, redraw the circle on a separate sheet of paper, or download a blank version to work from at *www.selfcare101book.com/bonus*. If you use a separate sheet of paper or the downloaded copy, I recommend that you complete it and then keep it folded inside this book to refer to as needed. Be sure to include your name *and date* for future reference. As you begin to implement the other tools presented, you can come back to this exercise and do it again with a new circle to see your progress. You'll be amazed to see how it can change shape in a short of amount of time when you are truly focused on making powerful self-care-centered changes in your life.

CIRCLE OF SELF-CARE ASSESSMENT
INSTRUCTIONS

Place a dot **on the line** in each self-care category to indicate your level of satisfaction with each area. Place a dot at the center of the circle to indicate complete *dissatisfaction* or on the perimeter of the circle to indicate complete *satisfaction*. Most people fall somewhere in the middle (see example).

Connect the dots to see your Circle of Self-Care.

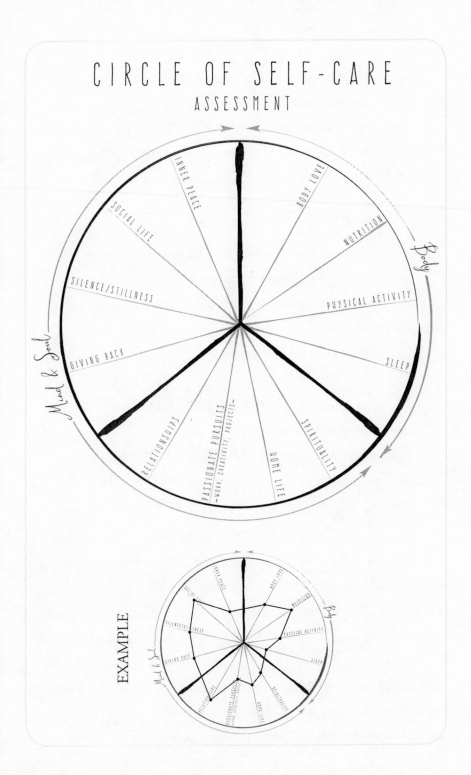

CIRCLE OF SELF-CARE
ASSESSMENT

EXAMPLE

To analyze your results, if all of your dots made a perfect circle on the outer perimeter, it would suggest that you have mastered perfection in managing your self-care needs and absolutely nothing could be improved upon, which is obviously highly unlikely. I suspect not even the Dalai Lama would mark it that way.

Now, sit back and review where your responses landed and the overall feeling you get when reflecting on the shape of your circle. What areas need more care? What imbalances showed up for you? Does that seem consistent with where you are feeling the most uneasiness in your life?

Write down your immediate thoughtful reflections to these questions on the assessment sheet to keep for future reference in case you come back to use this tool again. It's always great to celebrate our progress.

As I am certain you discovered by completing the Circle of Self-Care assessment, it's easy to chug along in our lives without any true sense of how well we tend to our personal self-care needs. It's also easy to have little or no understanding of our *actual* personal self-care needs. Perhaps you are at a point in your life when you are ready to take a good look at where you are and how you might be able to navigate this journey differently. Most likely, you are also looking for support, maybe even recognizing that unless you tend to your truest needs in a more self-honoring way, you may begin to experience issues in all other areas of your existence that will negatively impact your work, family, and relationships. Whether you've begun to have a sense of this or not, I can assure you that self-care is absolutely critical to every single aspect of your life. It's the root from which everything else can grow. Yes, it's *that* vital.

For that reason, I invite you to take a moment here to pause and consider some self-care questions. They will allow you to reflect on your current self-care needs. As you answer each question, you're also beginning the internal commitment process to embark upon your self-care journey. Please grab your self-care journal and take a moment to sit quietly with yourself and consider each of these questions with as much conscious intention as possible. I assure you that your answers will be quite revealing. As with the Circle of Self-Care assessment tool, you can use these questions as a go-to when life is feeling out of balance and you are craving a deeper connection with taking care of yourself in more empowering ways. They can help you reflect, get reconnected, and "begin again." We often need to begin again.

SELF-CARE REFLECTION QUESTIONS

This is where your self-care action plan begins! Give yourself some time to connect within. Be thoughtful with your answers to these questions. Keep in mind that you are gathering information here to bring more awareness to where you are *right now*. Do your best to avoid self-judgment, blame, or shame as you look at your current beliefs and what you desire for yourself in the future.

How would you describe the difference between self-care and self-indulgence?

Does self-care seem selfish? If so, why?

Do you believe you deserve self-care?

When you think of your own self-care needs, what activities does that include for you? Write down everything you can think of. Consider things like sleep, physical activity, nutrition, time with friends and family, meditation, stillness, alone time, etc.

Next, prioritize these needs, labeling the #1 most important need first. Then, go from there and label each one in priority order. I know this can feel challenging, but this exercise provides a tremendous amount of clarity, bringing into focus where you need to put your energies right now.

Now put a big circle around your top three and reflect for a moment on what it would take to tend to them. What adjustments would it take in your day-to-day living to truly nurture those needs? Don't get overwhelmed here, simply jot down some initial thoughts. We will continue to explore further as we move along.

PREPARING YOURSELF FOR THE JOURNEY

Any type of transition to something different requires a readiness factor. So give yourself a big hug right now and prepare to step back into your power. For this journey, you need to be prepared to move through blocks and blind spots, and get comfortable with change. After all, like it or not, discomfort is an inevitable factor for growth. It's important to note too that change doesn't always have to be a tidal wave. In fact, true transformation is generally accomplished with many mini-steps. Therefore, in our approach here, we will be addressing small, incremental habits throughout this process, which ultimately lead to big transformation. To get the most out of this experience, you'll need to be open to trying on new habits that will undoubtedly not only serve you well today but for the rest of your life. Also, know that you can absolutely adjust as you go. That's part of the journey, too.

Additionally, settle into the fact that this work is not something you do and simply check off as done. It's bigger than that. It's a way of life. It is a continuous process of doing, contemplating, taking more inspired actions, reflecting, and adjusting to suit your current needs. If you take consistent action, shift your perspective, and see the opportunity to do this work as a gift, I guarantee that you will reclaim yourself in the process. Have you ever heard the saying, "Discomfort may happen in our lives, but suffering is optional"? That's absolutely true with self-care work. Don't expect to live a life that is void of all challenges. That's not real, but the suffering part is absolutely optional, meaning we get to choose how we react and respond and how we take care of ourselves through the process. As we expand on this journey, you will learn the immense power of connecting with your needs—today, tomorrow, and every day—so that you can create self-care habits that always serve you well. You will learn to be adept at following your own moving target as you get more and more clarity.

As you move into a bigger focus on self-care, it is important to give up what you do not control and make each day count. Your days will absolutely change when you are truly committed to your life and your wellbeing. Lifestyle transformation lives there. It allows you to get out of the trenches and into your real life. The movement towards true self-care and self-love begins with one tiny shift in the way you see yourself and in your awareness. Remember that transformation often begins with chaos. So, if that's where you are, let go of the need for certainty about where this process will lead you and trust that you will arrive at the exact insights you need.

One other factor to consider as you move forward is that while you are making self-care a priority in your own life, it is also critical to honor others' self-care needs as well. This is not about selfishness, remember? Knowing how meaningful this work is, you'll need to allow other people in your life to explore what they need and give them support along the way. You may even be their new source of self-care inspiration. In my own life, this can show up when I'm trucking along with my own prioritized self-care journey and then get stumped when my husband decides he needs to go on a fishing trip with the guys. *Wait, whoa, how can he do that when I need help with the kids over the weekend? After all, he has been gone all week and I'm ready for a break so I can take care of me.* If I'm not careful, this can quickly turn into trying to subtly "guilt" him into not going or, at the very least, trying to make him feel bad if he does. At times like these, we need to check in with ourselves through honest conversation and take ownership of each of our individual needs and how we can support each other best.

✌ SELF-CARE DARE ✌
A MOMENT OF PAUSE

Before moving forward, first be sure you have completed the Circle of Self-Care assessment and self-care reflection questions. Second, take a moment to pause and do something incredibly nourishing for yourself. You absolutely deserve it. Perhaps you could schedule some time to spend in nature, sleep in or go to bed earlier than usual, give a big and heartfelt hug to someone (you get as much benefit as they do), or buy yourself some flowers. Or, if you are up for some pampering, get a mani/pedi, a facial, or a massage. Then, enjoy and acknowledge that this is a precious gift to yourself, because it absolutely is and you are worth it.

part 2

← HONORING YOU →

"The only person you are destined to become is the person you decide to be"
- Ralph Waldo Emerson

CHAPTER FIVE
«— COURAGEOUS INQUIRY —»

Over the past few decades, we've gotten clear that the essentials of a healthy life include a whole lot more than nutrition and exercise. We now know that the total, sustainable self-care package also includes lifestyle habits around sleep, stress management, satisfying human connections, and a commitment to continued personal and spiritual development, to name a few. If we realize this, why then do we still struggle to incorporate regular daily habits that support all of these aspects into our whole-person wellbeing? My theory is that we get stuck on autopilot and forget to focus on the importance of self-care, until something critical happens in our lives, like a life-altering illness or an emotional rock bottom that comes as a result of being in a constant state of overwhelm.

My challenge for you is to acknowledge wherever you are at

this moment and make a commitment to continue to make self-care a priority in your life. As you navigate your own journey, you will undoubtedly blossom into a newer and more self-aware version of yourself. You might even surprise yourself with the peace, serenity, and wholeness that shows up. That is the ultimate goal. This work is like a launching pad for a new you, the 2.0 version who is ready to engage fully in all that life has to offer. Your body will feel better, you'll be energized, your mind will be sharp, and you'll experience your life, even the challenging parts, with more grace and grit than you thought possible. All of this without dieting or slugging it through a rigorous exercise program that you hate. I don't believe in either of those.

Just as we talked about in the last chapter, have the courage to stay committed to this process. No judgments allowed. Forming Team YOU will be unlike anything you've experienced before. Embrace it with open arms and allow this process of self-care to unfold.

Now that you've completed the exercises in the last chapter, I expect that you have a clearer sense of where you are emotionally and intellectually with regard to self-care. I am sure you have a deeper understanding of what self-care has meant to you in the past and possibly a new way of thinking about it now. Additionally, based on the Circle of Self-Care assessment, you have a big picture view of some areas where you can focus your initial energies to build your own self-care practices. From there, even before we begin to talk about specific how-to strategies, the most important thing we can do is work on mindset. In order to do that, some questions are in order.

One of the best ways to gain a clearer understanding of

where you are and where you want to go is in getting curious and asking questions. It's an incredible tool to get the juices flowing, to get unstuck and begin to explore possible shifts that will serve you better going forward. In fact, if the questions are potent enough, one conversation sprinkled with powerful and relevant questions can literally change a person's life. Questions invite you to engage at a different level and bring clarity to the process. Learning to nurture with self-care is partly about learning to question things. This is a crucial way to get in touch with what is right for you. You are allowed to ask yourself if this food, exercise, supplement, or prescription is actually *right* for you. Don't be afraid to question everything.

I invite you to begin to get curious about yourself. In gaining the ability to ask the most relevant questions, reflect on the answers you find, and then make adjustments based on your own insights will provide an invaluable tool and skill, not only as you begin building Team YOU, but in each stage of the process and beyond. Be a tireless toddler about your own questioning. Your answers are like gold nuggets that tap into your own wisdom and insights. From there, new understandings emerge. This further allows you to tune into your own frequency and tune out the static. If you are not used to this kind of work, be patient here, with yourself and with the process. Let's begin to explore. First up, *What is your why?*

WHAT IS YOUR WHY?

"If you have a strong enough WHY you can bear almost any HOW."

~ Nietzshe

The most powerful way to begin any new transformational effort is with a connection to your reason for wanting to engage in the process—YOUR WHY. Building your self-care routine is no different. The most important question you can ask yourself at this point is, "WHY do I want to do this work?"

So, why do you want to do this work? Dig in and swim around in that question for a minute. Think about what you want to feel like, look like, act like, be like, and live like on a daily basis. Your entire way of living a self-care lifestyle depends on your answers to this critical question. It's extremely important to complete this step. Do not skip it no matter how daunting it might feel. Connect with the power of *your why*. Get still and quiet, take several deep breaths, and really reflect on what that means to you. Connect with the emotions behind *your why*, not just on the outcome you are hoping to achieve.

Many of my clients have shown up to work with me with strong desires to lose weight, even though I'm very clear up front that I am absolutely not a weight-loss coach. If this is their motivation for seeking out my services, though, I honor it. My objective, however, is to move them away from that idea as their main goal and help them uncover their *real why*. I always begin a new coaching program with the powerful *why* question, so I can get a sense of their bigger vision—about what they believe this work together will result in and why that matters to them. I ask them to visualize and describe to me in great detail what they envision, adding as much juicy emotion into the mix as possible.

Most of my clients have shared that although they've gone through this exercise, they still secretly hope that whatever we work on together will ultimately lead them into a "smaller version" of themselves. While weight loss has been a side benefit of my coaching program, it is *not* the focus. But, I will tell you this. The secret to why they can still lose weight without harsh dieting and rigorous exercise is because there is a magic that takes place when you are actually tending to and nourishing your whole self in a loving and gentle way. The chronic inflammation, inherent in most of us living in modern times, can let go and your body can start to respond differently and work in harmony with the rest of you, shedding excess weight, water, and toxins. What an incredible gift to give your body.

One of the most impactful conversations I've had in recent years is an incredible testament to the possibilities that can result from the concept of courageous inquiry and reconnecting with our "why." However, I was absolutely not ready to have the conversation when it took place.

While still in my nutritional chef culinary program, I had the good fortune to be influenced by the work of Marc David, founder of the Institute for the Psychology of Eating in Longmont, Colorado. I read his book, *Nourishing Wisdom*, and attended several programs that he offered. During one of his all-day seminars, I had the opportunity to talk with him firsthand about what was going on for me personally. That conversation ended up being a total gift that I initially couldn't appreciate.

At the time, I was a competitive athlete in a sport called Figure Competing. It is a form of bodybuilding for women where we would lift weights, do cardio exercises, and eat a very specific diet to create the "ideal" physique—shapely shoulders, wide and muscular back, lean abs, killer legs, and a high and tight booty. Then, we'd train to lean out and peak in order to compete with other women who also trained like we did by presenting our hard-earned bodies to a panel of judges with a set number of poses. I'd like to add that while there are criteria for the judges to follow, there is also a certain amount of subjectivity involved. We got our ultra-lean bodies tanned to the absolute max with dark spray tan and then wore loads of makeup so our faces could actually be seen on stage. It was kind of like a beauty pageant on steroids (without any real steroids, at least in my case). We'd line up with other competitors, do our set poses, and get judged to see who had the most ideal physique in that minute, on that day. To this day, that six-year stretch was the most disciplined I've ever been about any single thing in my life. Discipline with a ginormous, capital D.

I shared with Marc David about how completely frustrated I was at that time. Although I was *extremely* disciplined *most of* the time, I still gained weight if I cheated on my strict diet for even one single meal. That's how sensitive my body was. It seemed crazy to me. I couldn't understand how my body could be so unforgiving when I literally had a part-time job in exercise and dieting. I recall that he simply challenged me with one simple question. "What do you think would happen if you let go of the 'dieting' mindset for a period of time and see how your body responds?" Then he added, "It's simple, you've created your body's resistance." *What is he talking about? How in the world did I create this?*

I thought he was insane to think that I would be able to release the dieting mindset. I mean, I had a show coming up right around the corner. If I released the dieting mindset and let myself just enjoy food again, I might actually fall apart. In this sport, there were silent badges of courage that were dished out on a regular basis for how many grams of protein you consumed and how little carbohydrates and fat went into your mouth. Of course, I thought he was crazy. He obviously didn't understand what bodybuilding was all about or how critical it was to eat exactly what you are supposed to eat, exactly when you are supposed to eat it. Even a single M&M would make me feel like a total failure.

While I could resonate with most of what he shared in his seminar and could see how it might be impactful for others, at the time I absolutely could not connect with his personal advice to me. It still stuck with me somewhere in the back of my mind, but it wasn't until I ended up completely and utterly broken down—emotionally, physically, psychologically, and in ways that I had yet to comprehend from my bodybuilding experience—and had begun my recovery that Marc David's words started to really resonate with me. Focusing so much on being and doing exactly what I thought I needed to be and do to be competitive in the figure sport set up my body to respond in a very certain way, without any forgiveness whatsoever. The process of courageous inquiry and my ability to explore my WHY for wanting to train and compete in that way was a big part of the discovery process to begin that recovery.

Now that I'm no longer living in that world and have committed some serious time to recovery and loving my whole self differently, I can see exactly why my body was so sensitive. I can't even begin to tell you how thrilled I am to be on this side of that entire experience. While I had never looked better in my life, I was literally dying inside, physically and emotionally. A big part of my passion and purpose today is to save people from the severely strict mindset I lived in that created disordered eating, severe body image issues, and literally tore up my body from the inside out.

My why at the time was intensely motivated by looking a certain way, which I believed would result from that type of training and dieting. Oddly, for me, it had little to do with a desire to actually be fit and healthy. The irony is that while I looked fit and healthy, my body was so depleted that it screamed out for my attention in various ways, like losing clumps of hair on a regular basis. Yet, I kept chugging along, pushing my body to the max, tapping into the deepest recesses of my inner willpower and powering through.

Reflecting back, I believe the body focus was greatly fueled by two key factors. One was my family circumstance at the time. I was a stay-at-home mom for five years and felt like training in that way with a group of women whom I connected with was an identity outside of my roles as wife and mom. The other, and perhaps even more of a driving factor, was due to the many social conditioning factors that most women face with regard to body and image. Societal pressures to look a certain way. Of course, I was also in it to win. Unfortunately, I ended up paying dearly, but that experience paved the way for an incredibly expansive journey to learn and grow.

Let's get started and uncover your *real why*. Turn to your self-care journal and begin by describing a day in the life of the newer version of you (You 2.0), with as much detail as you can muster. See it and feel it. Consider the following questions:

- ✔ What do you wear?
- ✔ What do you eat and how do you move differently?
- ✔ What time do you go to bed and wake up?
- ✔ Do you travel? Where to?
- ✔ Who do you spend time with?
- ✔ What do you do to contribute to the world?
- ✔ Most importantly, how do you FEEL? What excites you?

Take some time to journal your responses to these critical questions. There is immense power in being asked the right questions and making the time to reflect on them long enough to get your *right answers for right now*. This also gets you thinking with more of your senses and connects you more emotionally with your real why. It can't be just about losing weight. That's an empty why that can leave you unfulfilled, even if you reach specific weight-loss goals. It's not like your entire life will be completely Zen and perfectly perfect if you get to your goal weight or have certain measurements.

There are so many other happiness factors that need to be addressed outside of a specific number on the scale. So, if you think weight loss is your goal, ask yourself why you want to lose weight. What does that allow you to experience differently in your life? That's where the courageous conversation begins. Additionally, these questions can also surface beliefs and attitudes that may be preventing you from prioritizing your wellbeing. Take note of those as well if they pop up. Just note them, though. Don't hang on to them. To help you find your real why—the bigger more powerful reason why self-care is important to you—tap into it and move into that space with grace, loving yourself through the process.

~e~ SELF-CARE DARE ~e~

YOUR REAL WHY

Carve out time to complete all of the thoughtful *real why* reflection questions in this chapter. Then, take a long, deep breath, exhale, and settle in to knowing you are absolutely on the right path.

CHAPTER SIX

«— THE POWER OF CHOICE —»

Think about this for a minute. Every single thing in your life, every thought, every experience, the good ones and the lesson-learning ones, are there because you made a choice. Now that's powerful. You can choose to make self-care a priority or you can choose not to. You get to choose how this will go! You create all of it. You shape the experiences and you get to decide how you will interpret your progress. Step into the power of making a conscious, deliberate choice now, at the beginning of your work on building Team YOU. It is the most powerful action step you can take—in this moment, in each moment, of this journey, and for the rest of your life.

You choose. Say it with me: "I get to choose!" You get to decide what self-care activities are important enough to make you get up earlier or stay up later, and what healthy boundaries need to be set to help you stay focused on your intentions and goals. Do not buy into any of the negative stories you might be holding on to about the self-care choices you have made up to this point in your life. Do not let that define you in any way. The most important moment you have is this moment right now to begin a new journey and to tell a new story. Be a pioneer of your future, not a prisoner of your past. Ask yourself, "What experience do I want to create?"

Take a purposeful pause, breathe, take time to reflect, explore your inner dialogue, and really hear what you want. You choose. Do not blame your past or current self, any circumstance, or anyone else for that matter, for where you are now. Playing the blame game separates us from valuable insights about what it is we truly want. Harboring negativity is destructive and toxic and pulls us away from the vitality and wellbeing we desire. It keeps us at a "safe" distance from the support and authentic relationships that we need to help us manifest what we want. Choose a new path to walk. One with space enough to stop and look around and find the breathtaking view we seek to experience. Not choosing is also a choice. The power rests with you.

Your perspective can change everything. And guess what, you get to choose that as well, even if you have beliefs that hold you back. Simply choosing to see things differently makes all the difference in the world. You can view the opportunity to focus on self-care as a gift instead of a chore. You can give yourself permission to focus on yourself as a priority. In fact, as simple as it sounds, this is one of the most powerful things I do as a coach, teaching people how to give themselves permission to do this work by viewing self-care as essential, not optional. It makes the biggest difference in the world.

There is no prescription or order of musts in self-care, there is only the choice.

Choose to give yourself permission to take care of yourself. Stay in awareness of what your IDEAL day would look like if you could shape it to perfectly suit your self-care needs. To really love and support yourself, you absolutely need to start thinking in these terms. That is where our power rests. This is where we find our "natural" willpower, our inner voice, and our self-respect. We start to live on our terms—not in an attempt to be disrespectful to any other person, but in our own powerful way. We connect with our self-care superpowers to live on purpose instead of living in a fog, going through the motions in a pretend, someday life. Self-care is not a part-time job; it's your full-time responsibility. If you are dissatisfied in any way with your current life, commit to making the CHOICE to live differently. Nietzsche tells us that the snake that cannot shed its skin must perish. Prepare to shed your skin and prepare for breakthroughs. Own your experiences.

Making the choice to focus on self-care as a priority sets your entire energy into a new motion and direction. It becomes your focus. It becomes your reality, and as you get better and better, it will change everything about the way you start, move through, and end each day. Your commitments shift, your activities change, your body changes shape, your thoughts evolve, and you become more whole. What no longer serves you will be eliminated easily. And this changes your life completely.

MOVING INTO A CHOICE MINDSET

If being able to see all things as choices is a challenge for you, and it is for many, it's time to take a fresh look and move into a new way of seeing things. As a result, you will be able to apply this practice to making choices around what you need most to honor your self-care needs.

Let's take a look at an example. If, for instance, you are a single parent (or, like me, feel like a single parent most of the time), have small children at home, and you believe you need to stay home with your kids all of the time, is that belief accurate? If you also have a strong desire to spend time with friends in the evenings or go to an occasional evening event as part of your self-care nourishment, what choices do you have? First, identify that you are not stuck and that you do have choices. Then, get your thinking cap on and brainstorm your options. How can you move into a circumstance that serves you *and* your kids? Could you create a childcare trade with a friend perhaps, use a drop-in childcare service, hire a babysitter that you already know or interview new ones that could help, or could you possibly ask a friend or family member to watch your children? This is where you get to take responsibility for your needs and make choices that allow those needs to be fulfilled. There is always a choice. You can also decide to stay home, because the other options feel overwhelming. That's a choice, too.

Here are some questions that can help you move into a "choice mindset." Consider these as you reflect on each circumstance you'd like to change that will better support your fundamental self-care needs. In this case, a circumstance is any situation where you would like to take more self-care action, like sleeping more perhaps.

✓ Is there anything you see yourself doing or believing about this circumstance because "there is no choice"? If so, describe it.

✓ What are the options you have to address the circumstance? List all possible options. Get creative here and consider possibilities that may at first seem absurd. List anything and everything that could be a solution.

✓ Moving forward, what would be your ideal envisioned outcome for this circumstance?

✓ What are some immediate steps you can take to start moving yourself into empowered choice?

❧ SELF-CARE DARE ❧
DEVELOPING YOUR "CHOICE MINDSET"

Complete all of the questions regarding choice and note your responses in your self-care journal. Reflect on what shows up and use them as a reference as you work through the remainder of the book.

CHAPTER SEVEN
«— HEALTHY BOUNDARIES —»
SETTING THE STAGE

To stay truly committed to this process, setting up and maintaining healthy boundaries is a powerful step. This doesn't mean that once you set them up, they never change. Boundaries help us define who we are in relationship to others and they are a sacred part of an individual's self-care practice. Boundaries are the limits we set around our needs so that there is a clear message to others and ourselves about how we honor those needs. I also like to think of it as saying yes when we mean yes, no when we mean no, and giving ourselves some breathing room to figure out which it is. Personal boundaries are how we teach people who we are and how we would like to be treated.

Good personal boundaries protect you and help you connect with your true self. They are based on your beliefs, thoughts, feelings, decisions, choices, wants, needs, and intuitions. They are clear, firm, and, believe it or not, should also be flexible. Setting healthy boundaries allows you to connect with yourself and your needs. It allows you to feel safe, to relax, and to feel empowered to take care of yourself. Ultimately, when you don't protect your boundaries, your needs go unmet, which can lead to an onslaught of behaviors that are less than nourishing; not a desirable position if you are truly committed to self-care.

If you tend to have boundaries that are too loose, it might be all too easy to take on the emotions and needs of others, which often means foregoing your own. Additionally, people with boundaries that are too loose tend to be hypersensitive to others' comments and criticisms, are over-involved in others' lives, struggle with perfectionism and people-pleasing, spend way too much time trying to fix and control others with judgments and advice, tend to stay in unhealthy relationships, and take on too much work or too many commitments. When your boundaries are too loose you can feel responsible for everything and everyone, powerless, imposed upon, and ultimately resentful. Obviously none of this serves you well.

However, boundaries can also be too restrictive, which can lead to isolation and loneliness. You can set up structure, plan, goals, and programs that end up isolating you from staying connected to your own emotions and to other people in your life. By doing so, you miss out on life's goodness. The story I shared with you about how I had to eat and train to be involved in my competitive sport was an example of a boundary that was too extreme and too restrictive. I pretty much had no life outside of my sport, which ultimately stifled me from fully engaging in living. I didn't want to be around people who didn't understand what I was doing, or who might criticize my choice, or who ate freely and would make fun of how I ate, etc. It made socializing extremely difficult, so I didn't do much of it during those six years. And I didn't enjoy much in life, that's for sure.

Here are some signs* that your boundaries need adjusting:

- ✔ You feel unable to say no.
- ✔ You feel responsible for others' emotions.
- ✔ You are concerned about what others think to the point of discounting your own thoughts, opinions, and intuition.
- ✔ Your energy is so drained by others or outside circumstances and situations that you neglect your own needs (including the need for food, rest, etc.).
- ✔ You people-please.
- ✔ You are unable to make decisions.
- ✔ You hold a belief that your happiness depends on others.
- ✔ You take care of others' needs, but not your own.
- ✔ Others' opinions are more important than your own.
- ✔ You have difficulty asking for what you want or need.
- ✔ You go along with others rather than what you want.
- ✔ You are not sure what you really feel.
- ✔ You take on moods or emotions of others around you.
- ✔ You are overly sensitive to criticism.

Does anything on that list sound familiar? Do any of these describe you, how you feel, or how you act? It doesn't matter where you are with healthy boundaries at this moment. What's most important is that you begin to shift the way you see boundaries and then begin to establish healthier ones going forward. Be aware and make a choice to take a stand for yourself and to remain flexible as you grow. This doesn't mean that you draw a thick line in the sand and erect walls around you so tall that you become an island unto yourself. Instead, setting healthy boundaries will help you stay present and focused while you navigate into your new self-care way of life and will keep you empowered as you make continuous shifts. Plus, it will set the stage for knowing where you stand when others question what you are doing or comment that perhaps this work seems a little "selfish." Of course, by now, you know it isn't selfish, but that won't stop others from thinking it and maybe even sharing their thoughts about it with you. They are entitled to their opinion, but it doesn't have to negatively impact you or what actions you choose to take on your own behalf.

Start to become aware of your boundaries now and stay committed to honoring and updating them as you evolve. It's a key factor in your self-care success and it is truly a form of loving yourself. Here is the process to use each time you want to check in with yourself regarding your healthy boundaries.

EXPLORING SACRED BOUNDARIES

Know Yourself. Get cozy with your inner thoughts, feelings, beliefs, and needs. Without having a clear sense of these connections, you can't really know your limits. This will also help you more clearly define your needs when boundaries are crossed. One really powerful way to do this is to journal regularly, to stay connected with your inner world.

Be Flexible. Having healthy boundaries doesn't mean rigidly saying no to everything. Nor does it mean isolating yourself from others. We are constantly growing, learning, and evolving. Allow yourself some room to explore, expand, and be in the flow of what feels most right at the time.

Give Yourself Permission. Fear, guilt, and self-doubt are big potential pitfalls to setting healthy boundaries. We might fear the other person's response if we set and enforce our boundaries. We might feel guilty by speaking up or saying no to a family member or to someone at work. Many believe that they should be able to cope with a situation or say yes because they're a good daughter or wife or mom, even though they feel drained or taken advantage of. We might wonder if we even deserve to have boundaries in the first place. Boundaries aren't just a sign of a healthy relationship; they're a sign of self-respect and a very important part of self-care. So, give yourself the permission to set boundaries and work to preserve them. Give yourself permission to put yourself first, which gives you the energy, peace of mind, and positive outlook to be more present with others and to be there for them. When you're in a better place, you can actually be a better wife, mother, daughter, co-worker, or friend.

Notice and Then Release Any Judgment of Yourself and Others. Start practicing compassion and acceptance. When you can accept yourself for exactly who you are already, there is less need to hide your true self. A more positive inner world can help you feel safe as you navigate new self-care terrain. As soon as you hear that ugly inner mean voice showing up, stop, take a breath, thank it for trying to protect you from the paper tigers—those things that appear strong or fierce, but in reality are actually all show and no substance, weak, and nothing to be feared. Then, immediately shift into the kindest, most loving voice you've ever heard and re-tell yourself that same story with gentleness. Equally critical is practicing healthy compassion for others without the need to "fix" them.

Accept the Truth In What Others Say and Leave the Rest. Feel what you feel and don't take responsibility for or take on the emotions of others. Give back their feelings, thoughts, and expectations. Let everything else go. It isn't real.

Press Pause. Do you have difficulty saying no? Instead of letting guilt take over and replying with an instant YES, try saying, "Let me think about it and get back to you." Then, take *whatever time you need* to think about it and determine if it's something you really want to engage in before making the choice. When it comes time to share your decision, be honest about where you are, especially if the answer is no, and do not offer any excuses. You are *allowed* to say no and you don't *owe* anyone a detailed explanation. It can simply be that you respectfully decline and wish them the best with whatever it is. This was a massively difficult task for me, but as I practiced it, it got much easier. Now, it's a no brainer. This creates so much more space in life to participate in the activities that actually fill you up.

Pay Attention to Activities and People Who Energize or Drain You. Protect yourself by saying no to those who drain you, or find ways to reduce the drain by delegating and/or setting firm limits. Spend *more* time with activities and people who hold you to a bigger version of yourself and energize you. If you find that a person or circumstance is pushing you to your edges, hit the pause button and get connected with what you are feeling and why are you feeling it. What's missing from the situation and how can you best address it?

I guarantee that you know the answer if you really listen to your inner voice.

Here are some ways to address boundary setting:

▾ **Tune Into Your Feelings.** There are two key feelings that are red flags or cues that we're letting go of our boundaries: discomfort and resentment. If you are feeling either of these things, ask yourself, "What is causing this feeling? What is it about this interaction or the person's expectation that is bothering me?" Resentment usually comes from feeling like you are being taken advantage of or not appreciated. It's often a sign that we're pushing ourselves either beyond our own limits because we feel guilty (and want to be loved and accepted), or someone else is imposing their expectations, views, or values on us.

▾ **Practice Self-Awareness.** Again, boundaries are all about honing in on your feelings and honoring them. If you notice yourself slipping and not sustaining your boundaries, start by asking yourself what has changed. Consider: "What am I doing or [what is] the other person doing?" or "What is the situation eliciting that is making me resentful or stressed?" Then, mull over your options: "What am I going to do about the situation? What do I have control over?" Take new empowered action from there.

▾ **Be Assertive and Direct (and Respectful).** Of course, we know that it's not enough to create boundaries; we actually have to follow through. Even though we know intellectually that people aren't mind readers, we still expect others to know what hurts us. Since they don't, it's important to assertively communicate with the other person when they've crossed a boundary. In a respectful way, let the other person know what in particular is bothersome to you and how you can work together to address it. Obviously, not everyone initiates or receives direct communication in the same way. For you to take ownership over your self-care boundaries, you need to be as direct as possible with others about what you need, while being savvy enough to not disrespect their feelings either. Each circumstance deserves its own way of being handled. Take all of the factors into account and follow your intuition about what needs to be said and when. Then, have the courage to follow through.

Setting boundaries takes courage, practice, and support. Remember that it's a skill you can learn and master. And once you do, it creates so much room for exploring what you really want to experience.

One of the simplest things I've done for myself around boundaries is to remove all noise-based notifications from my smart devices. There are no more distractions that make me feel like I need to check my phone and respond immediately. I check my devices when I can and respond at certain times of the day. I had no idea how powerful this would be until I did it. I've taught the people who need to reach me the most how to penetrate the veil of notification silence, so they can reach me if and when necessary.

ᴇ SELF-CARE DARE ᴇ
BOUNDARY SETTING

Identify one boundary you'd like to set for yourself. Note it in your self-care journal along with one small step you can take toward honoring it. Remember, baby steps.

CHAPTER EIGHT

←— CLEARING THE CLUTTER —→

Clutter is one of the greatest thieves of clarity, focus, energy, and productivity. Clutter has a tendency to creep up on us. Letting go of things that no longer serve us is one of the healthiest things we can do for our mind, body, and soul. It also creates a fresh start for your new self-care journey. Some of my clients have found it extremely helpful to commit time early in their work with me to clear the clutter in their lives as a hat-tip to their impending transformation. I usually recommend it, and for some it's incredibly impactful. This not only clears their physical space, but also their minds and emotions, because clutter not only impacts you physically; it can also drain you psychologically. Research shows that if you are feeling stuck in some area of your life, start clearing clutter and notice how your mental clarity improves and your momentum starts to build. Have you ever noticed how much easier it is to get things done and think clearly when your environment is free of clutter?

Here are some considerations to make when you start clearing the clutter to prepare for a crystal-clear self-care commitment.* Whatever you do, though, do not avoid taking action on your self-care needs, even if you can't seem to wrap your mind around a clutter-clearing adventure at this time. This is an *optional* step that many people find helpful, but it is not essential.

Items you no longer use. Are you holding on to things you don't use? Of course you are. Look around your office, home, and car. What could you give away or throw away? Many people hold on to things out of fear that they will need them in the future. Perhaps it's a fear of not having enough. Don't allow that fear to cause you to stay in a cluttered environment that drains you. Release items when you no longer need them or use them.

Projects you are procrastinating on doing or completing. You may not think of it as clutter, but that old to-do list that keeps rolling over in your head every day is clutter for your brain. Either drop the projects, complete them now, or give yourself a new and reasonable deadline, then store them out of site until you can focus on them. If they stay stored out of site for a specified period of time, without you needing or wanting to look at them, toss them at your next clutter-clearing party.

Too much stuff in too little space. If you are one of the many who overstuffs your space (I'm raising my hand here), it's time to make room in your environment. From your desk at work to your bathroom counters, overcrowding your space can leave you feeling mentally overcrowded. When you make space in your environment,

Inspired by cbn.com/burton_clearclutter.aspx – Valorie Burton: Life Coach you make room for more of what you want in your life.

Mess, junk, and stuff that is in disarray. When things are completely out of order, it is more difficult to plan, strategize, think, or take action effectively. Before ending your day, take five minutes to put things in order—at work, home, and in your car—so that you can start fresh the next day. Make this a healthy habit and muster the discipline to maintain it.

Things you don't like. Is there anything in your car, home, or office that you simply don't like? Your environments should inspire you, not depress, frustrate, or irritate you. Make sure your environments are filled with the sites, scents, and sounds you love most. Create the desired feeling you want to have when you are in your spaces.

❧ SELF-CARE DARE ❧
RELEASING THE CLUTTER

Set a goal to spend two to three hours per day for the next seven to ten days to clear as much clutter as possible so you can start your self-care journey with a clear mind. If that schedule absolutely doesn't work for you, set one that does. Prioritize and start in the areas where you spend most of your time.

If you find yourself getting stuck on this dare, it's time to check in with yourself. Pay attention to the thoughts and excuses that may enter your mind before, during, or after you start a clutter-clearing project. If you are a bit of a hoarder, be gentle on yourself … some of your physical clutter may be linked to deep beliefs about yourself and your stuff. As you do your clearing and get to items you are not sure whether to release, notice how you feel in your body when you hold those items in your hands. If the item makes you feel low energy and has negative memories attached to it, trust your intuition and release that item. If it connects you to something positive, make a choice to keep it, but find a place for it that feels organized.

Once you've bagged and boxed everything you are ready to donate or toss, move those items out of your life as soon as possible so you can reclaim your space without any residual negative energy clinging to you. For items that you may want to sell, do that quickly also. Have your garage sale or list them for sale on an online site as soon as possible. Then, release them and move on!

CHAPTER NINE

‹‹— THE POWER OF PLANNING —››

W hile I believe that life unfolds exactly as it should, and ultimately
our needs are perfectly met in the process so that we can learn what
we need to learn to continue on our path of growth, I believe just as
much that in order to take true responsibility for our own self-care
needs, we need some structure and planning. Being a recovering
type-A perfectionist overachiever, I have to be careful here. I can
really get into some overly detailed planning. For our purposes, I
don't mean a rigid set of practices that is do or die. I mean a set of
intentions that honor your self-care needs like a sacred discipline.

Structure actually nurtures us and gives us safe room to play,
explore, learn, and expand. And it can hold us accountable to stay
on track. We will cover lots of ideas around thoughtful planning in
subsequent sections, but I want to take a moment to mention it here
in this section because I believe it's relevant and important.

RELEASING OUTCOME EXPECTATIONS

Before we even begin to discuss the nuts and bolts of creating your own self-care practices, it's important to introduce the concept of releasing outcome expectations. Know right now, up front, as you embark upon this new journey that you will be working diligently on getting in touch with your needs, setting boundaries, clearing clutter, determining what serves you best for mental, spiritual, and physical improvement, monitoring your progress, and ultimately, adjusting your plan as needed. You can put together the most amazing, awesome, best approach ever, and as you take action, you may find yourself impacted by something that you learn and want to change. The initial outcome you intend to achieve could end up looking very different as you experience and make adjustments on your journey.

I urge you to not get emotionally attached to a particular outcome, especially weight loss. It may end up being a byproduct of your efforts around self-care, but making it your focus and then checking every day to see where you are can lead to disappointment, not to mention continuous psychological distress. That is not our goal. The idea is to view this and yourself as a continuous work in progress, while still being able to celebrate each moment as perfection. Commit to the process and your progress, not the outcome. Create good habits around what it is you desire to experience and celebrate your commitment to the process. Shaming and feeling guilty are forms of self-sabotage that will not serve you. Shaming yourself when you don't do what you intended to do is the #1 way to demotivate yourself. View your experiences as *neutral feedback*. Reflect and adjust your actions as you move forward. Then run a new experiment and see how that goes. Reflect and adjust, following that cycle repeatedly as you grow.

Also, release the idea of and need for perfectionism in your body, eating habits, and self-care practices. You are exactly as you should be in each and every moment. It is possible to love yourself as is and still want to grow and learn new things to achieve new discoveries. That's our aim here. Honoring yourself in continuous new ways to nurture your own growth. Accepting what is while also embracing what can be. Be gentle on yourself and give yourself some room to expand into your new self-care journey. Try it on, see how it feels, and make adjustments as needed. And always know that you are a beautiful work of art!

❧ SELF-CARE DARE ❧
LOVE, ME

Write yourself a love note so you can refer back to it often as you move through and reflect on your new self-care journey. Write this note from this point of view:

FROM: The future rockin' self-care version of you

TO: The current awesome version of you

Let the "future you" tell the "current you" what the journey has been like, how it has changed your life, and why it's worth making the commitment. Dig deep and tell yourself all the things you wish someone would tell you about having witnessed your growth. Whatever you say, be sure to celebrate your awesomeness. This can be a long letter or a simple love

continued...

note written in a blank card. Keep it in your self-care journal or tucked in the pages of this book to reflect on often.

EXAMPLE:

Dearest Shelley,

I am so incredibly proud of you. You are living each moment in fullness, just as you intended. Committing to this journey is so worth it. You are such an inspiration and light for others. I am so grateful for your relentless commitment to continuous self-care and improvement and for following your passions and dreams, despite what sometimes feels like paralyzing odds. I appreciate your positive outlook and am absolutely in love with how you live as a model for the self-care practices that you teach.

Love,

Me

You are the only YOU you have. In this letter-writing process, one of my deepest hopes is that this will create a yearning for you, a fire for you to create more space in your life in every way possible, so that you can begin to shape your experiences with intention. Truly transformative shifts begin with a new commitment, which then inspires new actions. Committing to a lifetime of self-care not only will create more self-love, but it will also create more self-awareness and feelings of worth and accomplishment. It's a sacred contract with yourself. It's hard to put a value on that. It's priceless. No one else can prioritize your self-care needs but you. Give yourself permission and prepare to set yourself up for inevitable success.

The next step is to evaluate more thoroughly exactly where you want to begin to nurture your body, mind, and soul. Take a deep breath, reflect on everything you've learned and accomplished in the activities in this section, get a cup of tea, and let's get to it.

part 3

← NOURISHING YOUR →
BEAUTIFUL BODY

Our body is precious. It is our vehicle for
awakening. Treat it with care.
~ Buddah

CHAPTER TEN
«— LOVING YOUR BODY —»

Our bodies, minds, and souls are tightly interconnected to create our ultimate human experience. One influences the other profoundly to shape our belief system, which then influences how we feel and act. While I do not see them as separate entities unto themselves, I will address them separately in our discussions, because there are specific ways that we can nurture each of these elements to create a sacred synergy among them. Because people tend to view their "body" as a primary focus in self-care, we will explore that area first, then, in the next section, we will look at ways to nourish your mind and soul.

Many of us are dealing with body issues. It could be a particular disease you are battling, fatigue, or random aches and pains, whether from an injury or something more chronic. If your health fails, it can overshadow everything else that's going on in your life, including any sense of happiness and your level of stress. If you have a genetic predisposition for a particular disease, taking consistent empowered action with your health and wellbeing can actually help you defy your genes and reduce your risk of some diseases.

Perhaps you are struggling with body image and/or how you wish your body could look or perform. I believe that most people have no idea how good their body is designed to feel and function. As our bodies age, many of us start to believe that whatever is showing up as "signs of aging" are supposed to be there because we are aging. You accept what is at a certain age and just chalk it up to aging. In reality, our bodies can "age" so much differently if we intentionally care for them. The ultimate way to live would be to love your body and yourself enough to *want* to take care of it.

While it might not feel like it at times, you have tremendous control over how your body looks and feels, simply by the way you care for it. That control is rooted in your beliefs about your body and what ailments you are nursing. Are you the ailment or do you *have* an ailment? There is serious power in how you answer that question. People can begin to identify with their symptoms as something that IS them, not something that they HAVE. What you believe to be true is your reality, and your reality is different from any other person's on the planet. This is when it's time to get real and take a look at what is actually influencing the way you look and feel. How are you truly identifying with your body? Is it a priority to take care of it or does it feel like a burden? Are there things you can do to create a different relationship with your body? If you are human, the answer to that last question is YES.

If beating yourself up with the inner critic in your head

actually led to change, you'd already be perfect. Give yourself a break for a moment, invite yourself into open-mindedness, and allow yourself to see things with a fresh perspective, so you can begin a new journey with how you treat your body. This can be a difficult task, given our lifelong conditioning, but it's the most powerful way to move forward. Make a commitment to the idea of seeing your body differently or at least be open to seeing it in a new way. Become a partner and ally with your body and begin the journey of feeling at home in it. Identify and release the internal pressure we put on ourselves and the external pressure we receive from society with what we see in the media, magazines, movies, TV, and other cultural expectations. If you need healing in this area (and most of us do), allowing yourself to see your body with new eyes actually opens you up to a different access point for healing. After all, loving your body only when it is perfectly fit is like only loving your children when they behave perfectly. While there are many ways to measure "health," true healing is subjective, based on your own internal experience and how you notice where you are in the process. If you feel stuck in some way when you consider how you feel about your body, healing your thoughts and taking new actions is the most powerful antidote. The two most impactful choices you have when faced with any roadblock are to change your actions or change your mind. And guess what? *You get to choose.*

For many people, a big part of their resistance to caring for themselves and their bodies is that they are too busy. It's an epidemic. The first critical step in recovering from busy-itis is to stop using that word. When you believe you are too busy, you will always be too busy. It's a frantic mindset. This is where a shift in perspective is crucial. Make a choice to change your mind about being so "busy" all of the time. Choose a different story. Use a different word. I like to use the word productive instead of busy. That changes the busy mindset immediately. Equally important is not to perceive your self-care commitment as overwhelming. Change your perspective and see it as a gift. This is for you and for every single person impacted by your existence. Truly caring for yourself changes everything. It creates a different filter from which you experience everything else in your life. Once you get into the swing of things, you'll actually create more space in your life to tend to other things that nurture you.

This section focuses on why nourishing your body is important, and I will share a plethora of ways in which you can do that. Not to overwhelm, but to inspire. Do *not* feel like you have to tend to each one of these activities, especially not all at once. The idea here is to connect with what's real for you right now and take baby steps to create sustainable new habits that actually feel natural in your life, not forced. After all, your self-care process is about addressing your particular areas of interest and needs in a way that honors where you are at each period in your life. It's an ever-evolving process.

❧ SELF-CARE DARE ❧
YOUR BEAUTIFUL BODY

List five things you love about your body, as is, right now! Send your beautiful body a dose of gratitude.

CHAPTER ELEVEN

<< — ADDRESS NAGGING AILMENTS —>>

We all do it. We have some random, or maybe not so random, pain or discomfort lurking in our bodies, but we push it back and ignore it, hoping that it will go away. Luckily, sometimes it actually does. What I want to address here are the ailments that have been sticking around for a while that you *know* are not going away without further investigation. What is your body screaming at you to fix? It's a massively critical part of your commitment to self-care, and I want to inspire you to get on it. I know, it's a pain to try and make time in your schedule to get that chronic condition checked out, and there might be fear around how much time it will take up in your life to actually tend to it.

I've had plenty of times in my life when I've had to nurse chronic conditions, and I know it can feel like a part-time job to nourish your body back to health, but it's also a vital step in the self-care process. You need to know if it's something serious that might require extensive treatment or if it's an easy fix, but you obviously won't know unless you take action. Once you step into action, it can also begin to release the stress, anxiety, and worry that can build up from knowing in the back of your mind that you need to deal with the situation in some way but have been denying or pretending it didn't exist. There is incredible value in that step alone.

Let's look at how to stay empowered as you begin this process. If you are anything like me, you've had a bad experience or two with doctor visits, so let's get you laser focused on a way to proceed that lets you own the process.

First, get the routine tests you need. Update your blood work. Get a physical. Get the mammogram. Check in with the gynecologist annually, as recommended. Don't ignore these routine action steps. Make your physical wellbeing a priority. Doing these annually actually orchestrates all of the other areas of self-care.

Take the time now to book the appointments that you need. Get a first opinion, or a second opinion if necessary. Then, no matter what kind of practitioner you plan to see, prepare for the appointment so you can get the most out of it. If it's a traditional doctor, chances are that you will likely have less than fifteen minutes to spend with them in an appointment. Take care to get what you need out of your brief time together. Doctors are not there to make decisions for you. Take ownership of the process and look at your appointment as the opportunity to collect expert input. Then, you get to decide what's best for you.

PREPARING FOR YOUR APPOINTMENT

√ **Keep a symptoms diary** – you might think you
will remember the details about your symptoms,
but chances are you won't. Note things like when
and how the symptoms began and what makes
the condition worse or better. This makes it far
easier for both you and the practitioner.

√ **Prepare a list of questions** – take the time to write
down the questions you have and be sure that *all* of
them get covered during your appointment. If you
are seeing a doctor and they run out of time for your
questions, ask to speak to someone else in the office so
that all of your questions are addressed *before* you leave.

√ **Medications and supplements list** – prepare a list of
any medications (prescriptions and over-the-counter) and
supplements you are taking, including names, dosages,
frequency, and *why* you are taking them. Also, note any
side effects you might be experiencing, as well as which
medications and supplements you believe they relate to.

√ **Surgeries and invasive medical procedures** – list any
surgeries you have had in your lifetime and during the
past few years. Include any invasive medical procedures,
too, such as particular tests you've undergone. Note why
you had any of these procedures and the outcome.

√ **Take notes** – prepare to take notes during your
appointment. Bring a notepad and take whatever notes
you need so that you can remember the key elements of

your discussion. Record actions that they recommend
and things that you need to consider for treatment ideas.

You'll likely be completing a medical history that will ask you
even more questions, but having the above items prepared in advance
will not only help you connect with what you are experiencing, it
will be immensely helpful with completing the medical history once
you are in the doctor's office. It will also aid the nurses and doctors in
their evaluation. Whatever you do, be honest about everything. That's
the only way to get the absolute best evaluation possible. It's your life.
Own the process here. Take everything into consideration, and then
you get to choose the best course of action for you to take, given what
you've learned.

ᴥ SELF-CARE DARE ᴥ
YOUR MEDICAL CHECKUPS

Consider what regular physical checkups you are due to
have completed and get them scheduled. Also, if you are coping
with something more serious, but you are not sure where or
how to begin with a specialist, schedule an appointment with
a general practitioner as a starting point and get the process
moving to address it.

CHAPTER TWELVE

« — FEEDING YOUR BODY. —»
MINDFUL CONSUMPTION.

E very time you put something in your mouth, you make a choice about how you will fuel and treat your amazing body. How we nourish our bodies is one of the power centers for our entire wellbeing. While we know that total self-care is far more than just what's on our plate, our physical bodies are sustained by everything we put into our mouths. There is an opportunity to nourish ourselves both physically and emotionally each and every time we eat, drink, or take anything.

My philosophies around feeding our bodies are not about calorie coaching, and I don't subscribe to any one particular way of eating. The foundation of my work is steeped in a concept called bio-individuality. This philosophy supports the idea that there is not one single way of eating, or one formula or process that is right for every single person. For instance, maybe you heard about a particular way of eating that sounded great in theory, and your best friend was getting great wellness results by eating that way, but when you tried it for a week, you started to feel weak and bloated. Obviously, that way of eating isn't right for you.

We are all unique. We each have subtle differences in genetics, body type, culture, and environment. All of these elements can affect our food preferences and what is "best" for us at any particular time. Your food choices and eating habits are impacted by many factors. These include your personal history, family history, and culture; your schedule and time constraints; whether or not you work; your personal or family budget; whether or not you have kids; your preference to cook for others or for yourself, and whether or not you even like to cook; your age and activity level; as well as whether you are pregnant, nursing, or training for a sport; and what season of the year it is. How in the world could I tell you what you *should* eat with all those factors to consider? And this is not even a comprehensive list! What works for one person absolutely may not work for the next. Even if you get a rhythm and flow going around an upgraded way of eating that feels supportive, that way of eating can change over time as well, depending on the same factors noted above.

With these thoughts in mind, it's time to start connecting to what you and your body really need. If you can connect with the signs and signals that your body emits, you will realize how incredibly smart it is. Trust it and allow it to guide you to the foods that best support your health. It actually knows what to eat. It's our brains that struggle. When we get stuck in dietary dogma, we tend to ignore and dismiss what our body really needs. Remember, your body wants to feel good and it sends you messages through discomfort or food cravings that need to be decoded. The real issue is whether you're willing to listen and love your body in return.

As I said earlier, no one "diets" when they coach with me. In my opinion, "diet" is a naughty four-letter word, the "D-word." I spent a significant amount of time dealing with dieting, namely, when I was competing, which landed me smack in the middle of disordered eating that took me years to recover from. I know that the connotations around the D-word can create a mental crap storm of negativity and it can be a very touchy subject for some of us. However, you can't deny that what you eat is one of the most obvious ways to nourish your body. To figure out what serves you best, where you are right now at this moment, a little self-experimentation is needed. Think of it as creating a way of eating that is tailor-made just for you and your body chemistry.

Commit to start small and try on new approaches to an upgraded way of eating until you find something that you enjoy and that you can stick to for long enough to truly evaluate how your body, and emotions, respond. For instance, it might be eating a fresh salad of mixed greens for lunch during the weekdays or drinking your bodyweight in ounces of water every day. In considering you, your lifestyle, your body, and the many factors noted earlier, what might be a better way for you to eat that supports your body? What way of eating makes you feel energized? What way of eating makes you know you are taking care of yourself? The best way to eat for YOU is the one that gives you the desired results you seek. It is also the one you can stick with long enough that you can actually track some progress. I trust that you already have good ideas about where you might start.

Spend time connecting with what's right for you, given your goals and your life circumstances. Find a starting point, take action, and adjust from there as needed. Do not overthink this. Treat it as an experiment.

What I'm suggesting here is ideal for someone who is getting started on the process of self-care transformation to nourish their bodies. It's an ease-into-it approach that lends itself to better outcomes in the long run. If, however, you have very specific goals around weight loss or disease prevention, I recommend that you work with a professional who specializes in your goal and can help you reach it. Those types of programs are typically more aggressive in nature and require a specialist to help you monitor your progress.

Let's take a look at some *gentle* guidelines to consider when analyzing and thinking about ways to elevate eating that support your amazing body. This is not intended to be a set of rules. These are guidelines meant to encourage you to start listening to your body, to treat it with loving kindness, and nourish it with what it truly wants and deserves. Before we jump into the specific guidelines, let's go over a *grounding* concept of how to honor your body with food. Shifting your perspective to the idea that eating is a way to honor your body is a powerful practice to connect with how you fuel it. Some ways to enhance this connection are slowing down to eat, only eating while sitting at a designated eating area (not in your car or standing up), and taking a couple of deep breaths, giving thanks, and thoroughly enjoying each bite. If you can focus some energy on practicing these philosophies, it not only takes on a new mindfulness about the way you eat, but there are physiological benefits as well, like better digestion. Start here always.

Use the following guidelines as a platform for evaluating where you are with your nutrition at the present time and where you want to make some upgrades. These represent nutritional philosophies most of the nutrition world agrees with. They are fundamental concepts. And quite honestly, if you only focus on these principles, you could nourish your body extremely well without much additional input.

Hopefully this list inspires you, but don't over-complicate it. The overall goal is simply to get you more conscious and mindful about how you are fueling your amazing body. Read the next section and see what connects for you with small ways you can make adjustments to nourish more mindfully.

NUTRITIONAL GUIDELINES THE EXPERTS AGREE ON*

Eating More Vegetables Can Only Benefit You. And the Greener the Better! Vegetables, especially fresh and seasonal, have more vitamins and minerals packed into them than any other whole food. In fact, they are among the most nutritious foods in existence, calorie for calorie. They are high in fiber, vitamins, minerals, antioxidants, and thousands of trace nutrients that science is just beginning to uncover. Numerous studies show that eating plenty of vegetables is linked to a reduced risk of almost every chronic disease. Vegetables contain lots of fiber and make people feel full with a low amount of calories, still leaving you feeling light and energized. *The bottom line is simple—eat more vegetables.* Find creative ways to add more vegetables to your life. Personally, I make vegetables a part of every main meal of my day, including an omelet for breakfast, a big fresh main dish salad for lunch, and a protein with a vegetable side for

*Inspired by http://authoritynutrition.com/11-truths-in-nutrition-that-people-agree-on/

dinner. If, for some reason I can't get my vegetables in, I mix up some highly concentrated greens powder with water and chug it.

Whole Foods are Better than Processed Foods. There is a growing consensus that manmade, processed foods are harmful. Humans evolved eating unprocessed real and whole foods. They retain more of the nutrients and fiber, since whole foods are found in their natural state. Most highly processed foods don't really resemble real food at all. In my nutritional chef culinary program, we called them Franken foods or faux foods. Basically, they consist of refined ingredients and artificial chemicals, assembled in a package to look and taste like food, but they aren't real foods at all. Processed foods are harmful for various reasons; namely, they tend to be high in harmful ingredients like sugar, refined carbs, and processed oils, and are very low in vitamins, minerals, fiber, and antioxidants. What many people don't realize is that the food industry puts a LOT of science and effort into making processed foods as rewarding (and addictive) as possible. The way foods are engineered effectively short circuits the brain mechanisms that are supposed to regulate our appetite, easily leading to overconsumption. Excessive weight gain and metabolic disease start here. It is best to avoid processed foods as much as possible.

Added Sugar is Unhealthy. Added sugars, like sucrose and high fructose corn syrup, are harmful. No one is arguing about that fact. People mainly disagree on *how* harmful and *why* they cause harm. Some experts say that they are horribly toxic to our system, while others think they're merely a source of empty calories. Almost everyone agrees, however, that at the very least most people are consuming too much sugar and would be better off to avoid it.

Right now, the average American consumes about seventy pounds of sugar per year, and within those averages, many people eat one hundred pounds or more. Keep in mind that most people aren't deliberately consuming this much sugar. They're getting a lot of it from conventional, processed foods that have sneaky high volumes of sugar added to them. The best way to avoid added sugar is to read labels and familiarize yourself with the many names used for sugar. Evaluate where you are with your sugar intake, and take action to make reductions if you are over-consuming. There are entire sugar-busting books and guided programs out there to help, too.

If You Are Going to Eat Starchy Carbohydrates, Choose Whole Grains. Carbohydrates are somewhat controversial. Some people think the majority of our calories should come from carbs; others believe that they are completely unnecessary and may even cause harm. But even the most extreme low-carb warriors agree that *unprocessed, unrefined* carb sources are, at the very least, *less bad* than their refined counterparts. Refined grains, for example, have had the bran and germ removed from the seed. Those missing parts contain most of the nutrients and also have the fiber that mitigates the blood-sugar-raising effect of the carbs. When you remove the fiber, the carbs spike blood sugar and insulin rapidly. This leads to a subsequent drop in blood sugar, making people crave another high carb snack. This is one of the ways that refined carbs stimulate overeating. There are numerous studies showing that consumption of refined carbohydrates is linked to obesity and many Western diseases. If you're going to eat carbs, stick to whole, unprocessed sources that include fiber. And remember that you get to be the judge of how your body tolerates starchy carbohydrates.

High Quality Fats Are Essential. Do not fear fats! They are absolutely essential to a nourished body. The cells of the body are made of fat, and together with protein, they constitute the structural framework of your entire body. Fats help repair the cells of the body, which we all need. They transport vitamins to the cells, help maintain body temperature, aid in manufacturing hormones, give us energy, and help regulate our moods. Also, fats carry the flavor of foods particularly well, which allows the body to register the message "I'm full" more quickly than when eating other foods. The more high quality fat that is in the food, the longer it takes to digest and the longer we feel full in between meals. Additionally, fats actually slow down the release of sugar into the blood stream via the digestive tract, improving the way our body processes any sugars that were in the meal. High quality fats help to curb cravings for sugar and junk foods, too. Since you honestly can't eat too much fat before feeling really full, it's difficult to over-indulge in fat if you are truly consuming a high-quality source, as opposed to the low-quality hidden sources of fat in processed foods. A little high-quality fat goes a long way! How much "should" you eat? As I've explained previously, I'm not going to prescribe anything. My only recommendation is simply to be conscious of getting more high-quality fats in each day.

High-quality fat sources include cold water fish (such as tuna, salmon, and sardines), nuts (including nut butters and oils), seeds, free-range organic eggs, avocado, organic butter, coconut oil, olive oil, and avocado oil.

Getting Enough Omega-3 Fatty Acids Can Improve Your Body in Numerous Ways. Humans cannot produce Omega-3 and Omega-6. However, they are necessary for optimal function of the body and are therefore termed *essential* fatty acids. This means that we must consume these fatty acids in some fashion. The modern diet is low in Omega-3, but extremely high in Omega-6. This is a destructive combination, because eating a lot of Omega-6 actually increases the need for Omega-3. So, a focus on consuming more Omega-3s can make a huge difference in your health. Omega-3 consumption is linked to improved neurological health, including improved intelligence, reduced depression, and a lower risk of dementia. They also play critical roles in other cellular processes, such as inflammation, immunity, and blood clotting. The best way to get enough Omega-3s is to eat fatty fish and grass-fed/pastured animal products. If that is not an option for you, taking an Omega-3 supplement like fish oil is important. Omega-3s are also found in some plant foods, including flax seeds and chia seeds. However, the Omega-3s in plants are not nearly as potent as the Omega-3s in animal foods.

Hydrate More . . . with Pure Water. Water accounts for sixty percent of your body weight and is essential to every single cell. It hydrates your skin, promotes cardiovascular health, keeps your body temperature regulated, gives you energy, helps with muscle and joint mobility, and cleanses toxins from your system. Without enough water in our system, we become dehydrated, which means our body cannot perform these tasks optimally. You lose water when you breathe, sweat, and go to the restroom, and I am willing to bet that most of us consume far less than the ideal volume of water to stay properly hydrated. Even mild dehydration can drain your energy and make you tired. For your body to function properly, you must replenish its water supply by consuming beverages and foods that contain water. Yes, water and food both count in achieving your ideal hydration level.

Looking at the color of your urine is one way to know how hydrated you are. Light yellow or colorless urine typically indicates proper hydration, but dark yellow urine is a common indicator of dehydration. Your water needs vary, depending on many factors, but the basic rule of thumb is to drink at least half of your weight in ounces of water each day. Make it fun and create some great flavored waters with mixed and mashed fruit. When you feel thirsty, most likely your body is already insufficiently hydrated. While a great habit might be to drink a good volume of water first thing in the morning, it's important to sip water throughout the day as well.

Supplements Cannot Compensate for Poor Eating Habits, but ... If you take the first tip to heart and take action on consuming more real, whole foods, then you will be doing your body a great service in the area of nutrition. The composition of real, whole foods is incredibly complex. They contain way more than just the standard vitamins and minerals that you might be familiar with. Whole foods literally contain hundreds, if not thousands, of various trace nutrients, which have powerful health benefits. Also, the forms of vitamins, minerals, and trace nutrients they have is in a highly digestible and usable form for our bodies, unlike when we take a supplement, where only a small portion is actually digested and usable. Science has yet to uncover many of these nutrients contained in our whole foods, and modern nutritional supplements are far from able to replicate all the nutrients found in foods. Although many nutritional supplements can have impressive benefits, most experts agree that they are not able to compensate for eating poorly. For optimal nutrition, the foods you choose to eat are by far the most important. Take care of your diet first, then add supplements to optimize.

However, having said all of that, because the quality of even our real, whole foods has deteriorated over time, even if we ate what we believed to be incredibly nourishing, with platefuls of vegetables at every meal, the fact is, we would still not be able to get the optimal nutrients from that food. Food quality and our own bodies' ability to digest and process nutrients play a major role in what is actually assimilated by our bodies. Given that, I do recommend a few basic supplements that can help optimize your health. It's like nutrition insurance. The supplements listed below are foundational. Most women need these. If you are trying to support something specific, you can add supplements for that as well. I highly recommend that you make the investment in working with a qualified specialist who can help you select any additional supplements based on your actual needs. They can also help you select high quality brands and assist with proper dosing for your body type. Supplement quality matters, a lot.

Multi-vitamin – Vitamins are nutrients required by the body for growth, repair, normal metabolism, and optimal health, but few of us get the right ones at the right levels. That's because no single food contains all the vitamins and minerals the body requires. In addition, the combination of eating on the run, high levels of stress, and consumption of highly processed foods can lead to nutrient deficiencies. Multivitamins provide essential vitamins and minerals needed to maintain optimum health. Taking a multivitamin daily helps ensure that you have your bases covered. Any high quality, whole foods multi is usually a good bet. Go for non-GMO, organic, and one that is free of dyes, additives, and colorings.

Fish Oil – EPA and DHA (the omega-3 fatty acids found in fish oil) have been linked to decreasing inflammation, supporting a healthy heart, mood, and mind, along with feeding gorgeous hair and maintaining healthy weight. As discussed, while it's best to get nutrients from whole food sources first, you'd have to consume at least two 3.5-ounce servings of fatty fish per week to get the optimal amount of fish oil. If you don't do that on a regular basis, then it's a good idea to take a fish oil supplement. A good starting point is a high quality supplement containing at least 600-1000 mg of DHA.

Probiotics – Probiotics are live beneficial microorganisms that are widely believed to support healthy digestion and immune function. These friendly bacteria are essential for gut health, especially considering that low-quality foods and medications can destroy probiotic activity, which can lead to lower immune function, yeast overgrowth, and digestive disorders. A broad spectrum probiotic that contains Lactobacillus and Bifidobacterium strains is best. Take daily if you have gas and bloating, or a few times weekly to optimize digestion.

Vitamin D3 – Vitamin D may be called a vitamin, but it actually works as a hormone. It is responsible for hundreds of functions in the body, from healthy immunity to strong bones. It helps to move calcium and phosphorus (important minerals for keeping bones strong) into the bloodstream. When your body doesn't have enough vitamin D, it will take calcium and phosphorus from your bones. Over time, this makes them thin and leads to conditions like osteoporosis. Low vitamin D has also been linked to several types of cancer, weight gain, depression, poor nutrient absorption, and low bone density. Vitamin D3 is the most bioavailable form (meaning most readily available for absorption in the body). The sun's rays, when absorbed by the skin, convert to D3 in the body; however, most Americans do not get enough year-round sun. The integrative internal medicine doctor I worked with shared that a vast majority of his patients were deficient. He used to test everyone for vitamin D levels, but after hundreds and hundreds of tests came back deficient, he simply started recommending it for everyone. If you want to be certain, though, you can have your vitamin D level tested. This will help you know just how much you really need. Ask your doctor to have your 25,OHD level checked. An ideal test result should be between 40 and 80.

If you feel particularly energy depleted, consider taking a B-Complex (includes a variety of eight types of B vitamins in one pill) – B-vitamins help the body convert food into fuel for energy; contribute to healthy skin, hair, and eyes, and proper nervous system functioning; maintain metabolism, muscle tone, and a sharp mind. Deficiency of certain B vitamins can cause a host of symptoms, such as anemia, tiredness, loss of appetite, abdominal pain, depression, muscle cramps, respiratory infections, hair loss, and eczema. B vitamins are essential for producing the energy necessary to meet the demands of everyday life, whether you're going to the gym, doing laundry, showering, or giving a presentation at work. Opt for a high quality B-vitamin complex with highly digestible forms of B vitamins.

The secret to all of the guidelines mentioned in this chapter is to try some new ways of eating and nourishing your body with supplements that better support your health goals, then check in to see how your body is doing. Ask questions such as, "Does my body tolerate this way of eating well? Am I digesting things okay?" If your body seems to struggle to digest particular items, take note. It could be time to work with a specialist to identify food sensitivities. Or perhaps a particular supplement could help. Take ownership here in a fresh new way.

⤷ SELF-CARE DARE ↲
FOCUS ON NUTRITION

Identify and write down what areas of nutrition you will focus on first to take baby steps on your new self-care path. Don't overwhelm yourself. Start small and identify two to three new ways to nourish yourself differently as a starting point.

CHAPTER THIRTEEN

← MEAL PLANNING GUIDELINES →

One of the areas that is a huge missing element and is extremely useful in making healthy, supportive eating choices is *meal planning*. I know it's not sexy or fun for most people, but it's necessary. Planning eases stress and actually creates more time and freedom in your life. It also solves the mind-numbing and continuous question of "What's for dinner?" Wouldn't it be nice to have a calendar of meals posted on the fridge so when anyone in your family is tempted to ask that question, you can point to the calendar?

Meal planning efforts are helpful, no matter how you plan to eat—whether you are cooking for yourself, cooking for the family, eating out, picking up healthy prepared food, using a meal preparation and delivery service, or packing food to take on the go. After reading the previous chapter, hopefully you know what eating upgrades you'd like to make. Having a plan will honor those desires and convert them into actionable habits. It helps you take ownership and not fall into excuse mode. It is the secret to minding the gap between the way you *want* to eat and what you are doing now.

Get everyone who eats food in your household involved in the process of planning. You can certainly share the responsibility of leading the planning efforts, too. You don't always have to do it on your own, unless you are like me and you actually enjoy the planning process. Get out a blank weekly calendar (or download the blank weekly meal-planning calendar from *www.selfcare101book.com/bonus*) to start the process. Then, somewhere on the calendar, note the dates of the week you are planning for. We'll focus on dinner meals in this chapter, since that is generally the most troublesome for people, but you can apply the same planning principles to other meals (and snacks) too.

Have your master personal and work calendars out so you can reference them as well. The first thing to note on your blank meal-planning calendar is any days of the week that you will not be eating at home. Make a note about where you will be and how you will handle your meal for that night, so you can pre-think through how you will honor your healthy eating objectives in that circumstance. If it's a business meeting and you know there won't be healthy eating options available, perhaps you will want to grab a salad and eat ahead of time or bring it to the meeting. If you are going out to dinner, check out the restaurant menu online ahead of time, so you will be prepared for things you can order that help you meet your goals. If you are going to someone else's house to eat, you might offer to bring a dish or snack, so you know you'll have "something" healthful to eat.

Allow yourself to enjoy the gifts (in the form of food) that they will be sharing with you, too. This is not about perfect eating, because that doesn't really exist. It's about conscious eating.

The second thing you'll note is days of the week that you will be eating at home, what you will eat, and how that meal will get to the table. Will you pick up something on the way home? Will you be using a meal preparation and delivery service and have the meals already stored in the fridge? Will you be making a home-cooked meal? Or perhaps your private chef will be preparing a delicious meal for you. It's possible, you know! If you are planning to prepare a home-cooked meal, do you already know what you want to cook or do you need some inspiration? If you are cooking at home, hats off to you. I truly believe that home cooking is one of the greatest forms of self-care and self-love.

If you need some menu inspiration, try starting with personal and family favorites. If you need something more, tap into the vast resources of recipe inspiration available online, in smart device apps, magazines at the checkout stand, or cookbooks. There is no shortage of recipe ideas for any little thing you might want to try. The public library is a great resource for cookbooks as well. I suggest copying all recipes that you want to try (or tearing them out of magazines) and starting a "recipe inspiration" folder that you can access when it comes time to plan. In that way, there are always fresh ideas waiting for you.

Grocery store planning is next. For time efficiency, I recommend structuring your week around going to the grocery store as little as possible. If you do it right, you might be able to get away with once per week. How does that sound? I also recommend that you do not shop on the same day that you do the meal planning. Schedule that to be on a separate day and assign it to another person in your household, if that's at all possible. If you can, spread the responsibility around to help everyone be involved in getting food on the table and to free up time for you to focus on other self-care activities. Keep a rolling list of items needed from the grocery store somewhere in the kitchen, where you and anyone else in your household can make notes on the list. Then, as you plan meals for the week and you know which recipes you want to prepare, add those ingredients to your rolling list. In that way, the list is ready for whoever is going to the store. You can download a blank grocery shopping list at *www.selfcare101book.com/bonus* to help with this process. It is the one I have personally used for years, even when I was grocery shopping as part of my profession.

As a final thought, if you want to be extremely time efficient with any meals that you are preparing at home, you can pre-cook them all in a few hours one day of the week, then store them in the fridge and re-heat when you're ready to eat. Of course, you can always prepare them on the night you will eat them. The choice is yours.

HERE IS AN OVERVIEW OF THE PROCESS WE JUST DISCUSSED:

When will you plan? Set aside a couple of hours each week to plan out your meals for the entire week. Then, actually block that time on your calendar. I suggest making it the same time block each week. I like to do this on Friday afternoons. That seems to fit best for me, since I am the one who does all of the meal planning in our home. While I've handed over other parts of the process of getting food on the table to other members of my family, I still own the planning piece, and for now, I wouldn't have it any other way. You can plan for more than one week at a time when you get the process down, but if you are just starting the planning thing, go for one week at a time.

Pick a day to do the grocery shopping for the week: Who's going shopping and on what day? Is the list ready to go?

Cooking for the week. If you plan to make any home-cooked meals for that week, consider cooking them all in a few hours one day per week. Many people choose Sundays for this task. Then, you will be prepared for the week with pre-made meals that you can pull out when you are ready to nosh. I recommend that you don't grocery shop and cook on the same day. It can feel like too much to do it all in one day. Spread the love and make it manageable. Decide what feels best for you and go!

OTHER GENIUS TIMESAVING HEALTHY EATING TIPS:

Buy in bulk. Buy high quality meats in bulk when they are on sale. Freeze and pull out the meat to thaw 24-48 hours before you need it for cooking a recipe. Also, stocking up on nutritious foods to keep around the house can help remove the temptation to eat mindlessly.

Make the most of your leftovers. Plan your meals so leftovers from dinner can be packed and eaten as lunch the next day. Chop up your chicken breast from the night before and add it to an omelet for breakfast or slice it and serve with mixed greens and veggies as a main-dish salad.

Eat breakfast for dinner. And vice versa. Get creative. Add chicken, whole grain rice, and vegetables to a breakfast omelet.

Order an extra meal. If you are eating out, order an extra meal to take home to eat for lunch or dinner the next day. This is do-it-ahead genius!

ᵉᵛ SELF-CARE DARE ᵉᵛ
MEAL PLANNING FIRST STEPS

Did you already create a new meal plan based on the ideas in this section? If so, celebrate yourself. If not, what aspects of meal planning resonated with you most? Which will be most helpful? When will you begin taking new actions around meal planning and how? Get some clarity on your thoughts, get your planning pants on (if there is such a thing), and move into action.

CHAPTER FOURTEEN
⟨⟨— MOVEMENT MATTERS —⟩⟩

Unless you live under a rock, and I doubt that you do, you are aware that having some regular physical activity in your life is beneficial. It is just a fact of human existence. Physical activity is beneficial. Period. No one can dispute it. Regular physical activity has a multitude of long-term health benefits, and every single person on this planet can benefit. Heck, even if you are incapacitated in some way, it is highly recommended that you participate in regular movement—even if it is done for you with the help of a physical therapist. Just to get us on the same page, here are some of the benefits of regular physical activity:

     ✔   Controls weight
     ✔   Makes you feel better about yourself

✔ Enhances mood

✔ Combats stress

✔ Boosts energy

✔ Promotes better sleep

✔ Improves your sex life

✔ Combats health conditions and diseases

✔ Increases your chances of living longer

✔ Helps you stay mobile

✔ Builds stronger muscles and bones

✔ It can even be FUN, perhaps a way to socialize too

I am sure you've heard this stuff, right? We all know that physical activity is beneficial, but many of us, including myself at various periods of my life for various reasons, do not participate. Knowing that it is beneficial is not enough to get us moving. There is so much more to it than that. It is far more about having the desire and motivation to do it. So, where does that come from?

First, refrain from using the word "exercise." Exercise conjures associations such as, "I have to," "I should," "I will one day, someday, maybe," to name a few. It can feel like a "pay your dues" approach that counts on sheer willpower for you to sustain it. For most of us, that does not last. When was the last time we got jazzed up about the idea that we *have to* exercise in order to [you fill in the blank]? That doesn't feel good. So, I do not use the word "exercise" when I am referring to the subject in my own head or when I am talking with my clients. That word alone can bring up a slew of issues, none of which are helpful in getting people to move more. We also want to avoid using the word "should." For anyone trying to focus on true

self-improvement, "should" is a very disempowering word. Perhaps
your family and friends can help here and point out whenever you
use that word. Do whatever it takes, because that word drains your
power. Instead, choose the word "could." The word "could" implies
choice. After all, as we discussed in the chapter all about choosing
you, there is power in making a choice. You always have a choice. You
can be physically active or not. It's totally up to you.

Instead of "exercise," the word I use is MOVEMENT.
The most powerful thing about that concept is that every type of
movement you do in your life counts. It is not just the intentional
physical activity you participate in when you go to the gym or go
for a run that counts. The word "movement" conjures up the idea of
possibility. The ideal way to shift your mindset is to view movement
as a *gift* that you get to give your body. Consider what energizes you.
And I do not mean only physical energy. I mean forms of movement
that truly energize your whole self.

Shifting to the concept of movement as opposed to exercise
was monumental for me personally. When I was training to compete,
I believed with my entire being that there was only one way to
exercise to achieve the body I was trying to shape. I paid a lot of
money to a trainer who specialized in this form of training to tell me
how to do just that, often to the detriment of my own inner knowing
about what *felt* right for me. I was often tired and injured, I felt like
crap emotionally, and had periods where my hair literally fell out
in clumps. The training program included about twelve to fifteen
hours per week of "exercise," including a combination of very specific
weight training and massive amounts of cardio training to stay lean.

I literally had a part-time job in exercise. After all, the leaner the better, especially once you hit the stage. When I was trying to peak for a show, I sometimes trained three times *per day*. Even in the "off-season," when I wasn't competing, if I did not stay lean to a certain degree, it was frowned upon as "falling off the wagon." Keep in mind that I *chose* to participate in this. No one forced me. Obviously, there was something about it that kept me in it for as long as I did. After all, I truly have never *looked* better in my life. But, like many sports, it is not something a person can do for their entire life. It is not sustainable. It is something some people try on at a certain period in their life. They experience it, learn from it, and then move on.

For me, it took a serious wakeup call moment that included being so physically, emotionally, and psychologically depleted that I blacked out on the freeway while driving with my kids in the back seat. Luckily no one was hurt, but this was significant enough for me to get real with myself about making a new decision that better supported my needs. I quit competing and commenced with a total body and mind repair, but admittedly, the training mindset was still seriously ingrained. The experiences I had with training and competing profoundly shaped my thoughts and beliefs around what *counted* for exercise. In fact, I think it was kind of an addiction. It took years for me to unravel it in my mind, and to some degree I am still working on my philosophies about what counts as movement.

There was a period of time after I decided I was not competing anymore and started repairing my body and emotions that I actually did not even walk fast for almost a year. I developed a loathing distaste for exercise and just could not bring myself to do it. Imagine that, hating exercise so much that you don't even walk fast for an entire year. I had come off six years of training twelve to fifteen hours per week and then just came to a screeching halt, because I could not even stand the thought of exercise. Plus, in my efforts to recover from how depleted I was, the practitioners I was working with at the time suggested that I rest a lot and only go for light walks as my form of movement while my body healed. In addition, I was nursing significant shoulder and hip injuries due to overuse. Although I had good "excuses" for not moving very much, I knew inside that I just did not want to exercise, especially because in my mind at the time, there was only one way to exercise that actually *counted*. If I couldn't wrap my mind around doing it that way, then I might as well not do it at all. Have you ever experienced that kind of limiting belief?

Once I had spent enough time in recovery from my training and competing days, a new reality set in, and that is where the *movement* mindset began for me. It's a *much more* powerful way to think about regular physical activity in your life, which is why it's the only way I think about it now. So, back to you.

Let's take a real honest look at our two options for movement.

OPTION 1: Accept that you do not want to do intentional regular physical activity and be happy with that choice. The biggest mental and emotional shift you can make is to see it as a choice and be done with it. Maybe you are recovering from something or nursing an ailment that will not allow you to participate in much physical activity right now. Or maybe, like I did for almost a year, you are struggling with your ideas around what "counts" as actual, real exercise and are protesting the whole thing. I get it. Give yourself permission to give it a rest and be truly okay with it. Take the responsibility and own it.

OPTION 2. Choose to take on physical activity, but do it with an entirely different mindset. Do not view it as "exercise." Instead, see it as *movement* and simply move your body more throughout the day. Every little movement that you do counts, and it can add up to big transformation over time, because it is sustainable. The secret with this formula is to find ways to move that connect with you and then just do it. You might even find joy in this process. Are you going to be a world-class athlete with this strategy? Not likely. But that is not who I am talking about here. I am talking about the rest of us. For most of us, movement matters and is all we need to focus on to get into a body-loving, sustainable self-care practice. Next, let's talk about the two ways to move more.

MINDFUL NATURAL MOVEMENT AND INTENTIONAL MOVEMENT

Mindful natural movements are movements you are already doing, but you make a choice to do them more. From the moment we wake up until the time we go to sleep, we are moving. Roll out of bed (abdominals/core), make your way to the bathroom (lower body), sit on the toilet (legs and buttocks), or sip coffee (biceps). Walking (mimics the treadmill), climbing stairs in your home or to access public transportation (imitates a Stairmaster), carrying children or groceries (simulates kettlebell exercises), or even sitting down and standing up (involves modified squats), are all examples of ways we move that simulate traditional exercise. We benefit from each of these types of movement.

The thought with mindful natural movements is to simply consider ways to move more throughout the day and make a mindful connection to that activity. For instance, you are already going to walk from a parking spot into a building. Instead of trying to find the closest parking spot, park in the farthest spot and walk farther (aka move more). Sometimes, you need to get from one floor to another in a building. Instead of taking the escalator or elevator, take the stairs. Many of us disconnect completely from movement and use it only as an option to get from one location to another or to accomplish an activity. By connecting and being present with that activity and your movement, you can monitor breath, actively decrease stress, improve the efficiency of the movement, and make a solid body-mind connection for long-term health. Become more conscious of the movement you are already doing on a daily basis and allow that information to set a solid foundation from which you can grow. Too many times we are being told we are not doing "enough" when the key is to recognize what we are *already* doing.

Intentional movement is about finding movement activities that you actually enjoy doing and creating *intentional* time in your life to do them on a more regular basis. The super-secret is that if you actually enjoy them, you will *want* to participate. Consider participating in a variety of movement types to maintain your interest and to keep the creative movement juices flowing. You might already know of some activities that you like. Let me encourage you to take a risk and try some things that feel new, too. You don't know if you will like them or not until you actually try something, right? Right. While I don't prescribe specific movement programming, since I believe you (and my clients) are quite capable, I will tell you that as a general goal, if you want to tap into the benefits listed above, aim for at least thirty minutes of intentional physical activity every day in addition to your mindful natural movements.

The question now becomes: What type of movement does your body want to do today? Let it come from your body and not from your head. The movement should be pleasurable, and remember, all movement counts. No one is *too busy* to find extra minutes here and there that can all add up. You can absolutely make this *fun*.

CREATING A MOVEMENT MENU

How about creating a movement menu? Does that pique your interest? This is an inviting way to participate in your life and set yourself up for regular, sustainable activity in life-centered ways to move more. You are perfectly capable of discovering and creating ways to move your body that feel good for you. You may find that you'll be drawn to ways you already move your body—walking, dancing, morning yoga, or taking the stairs. It's all good.

For starters, think of ways to move that make you happy. This is *the most* important step. Channel your inner child and reflect for a moment. Remember how those activities made you feel in your body? Light, free, fun, joyful, exhilarated. Notice where you feel that sensation in your body and let that sensation be your driving force for movement. Let your stream of consciousness flow. Kids move naturally without feeling bogged down by the idea of how much or how often they should move. Remember running, jumping, skipping, jumping rope, hula hooping, and riding your bike for miles without any particular place to go? Those were the days. However, as you got serious in adulthood or mobility became an issue, these activities may have been pushed aside. Well, I am here to give you absolute permission to make the good ole' days new again. The most beautiful thing about this approach is that it doesn't matter what your age, size, abilities, or interests—you can create a personal movement program that is enjoyable and suits where you are right now. Then, you can adjust *when* you want and *how* you want to stay involved in making this a healthy and sustainable self-care practice.

MOVEMENT MENU EXERCISE

In this exercise, you will be creating your own movement menu. Save it so you can refer to it whenever you need inspiration or a reminder of what you intended to do.

1. List every way to move that used to make you happy and that maybe you haven't done in a while.

2. List every way to move that you have wanted to try. For some additional ideas, download the MOVEMENT MENU IDEA LIST at *www.selfcare101book.com/bonus*. See the following page for some ideas to get you started.

MOVEMENT MENU IDEAS

NATURAL MOVEMENTS	INTENTIONAL MOVEMENTS
Parking farther from the door	Weight lifting and traditional exercise
Taking the stairs instead of the elevator whenever possible	Team sports
	Individual sports
Quick neighborhood jaunts, like visiting neighbors or going to the pool—walk or use a bike instead of a car	Pilates
	Yoga
	Jump rope
	Run
Quick grocery store stop—walk or bike	Walk
	Bike
	Rock climbing
Use public transportation—makes you walk more than driving everywhere, plus you are helping to preserve the environment since you won't be driving	Hiking
	Hula hooping
	Ice skating
	Dance classes or take dance breaks and jam to a favorite song
Wash your vehicle by hand instead of having it washed	Playing tag
	Frisbee
Use a standing desk or sit on a fitball instead of an office chair	Volleyball, badminton, baseball, football, tennis, golf
	Roller skating or inline skating
	Water sports (kayaking, water skiing, SUP, water aerobics, swimming)

Did you think of some movement activities that you would like to try? Did you see anything on my list that gave you any new ideas? I hope so.

STAYING MOTIVATED

The ideal situation is that due to the nature of the movements you are *choosing*, you will stay excited and motivated about maintaining your activity. Simply selecting fun new ideas to try and making a choice breathes new life into the idea of sustainable activity. However, as a human being, you might need an extra dose of fire under your behind now and then. For those times, here are a few ideas to stoke the fire:

- ✔ Recruit someone to join you in trying a new activity, even if it's once per week and even if it's a different friend each week. Pick a day of the week for your new activity and invite someone each time. It's always fun to share this journey with others. And it's a great way to stay connected with your buddies.
- ✔ Set an alarm at different intervals throughout the day to remind you to stay active. Maybe it's a reminder to take a five-minute walk and a stretch break every hour. This is especially helpful if you sit at a desk all day.
- ✔ Find a meetup group for a movement activity you *enjoy* and participate in their gatherings.
- ✔ Purchase an activity-tracking device that will automatically track your movement throughout the day. Some track steps, miles walked, floors climbed, etc.

- ꙮ For more specific movement training, sign up for a fitness challenge or sign up to participate in a race or competition that requires you to train in a specific way and that will provide that training guidance.
- ꙮ And if you just don't feel like moving, be okay with it. Give yourself a quiet moment of clarity and reconnect with your why. If that still doesn't motivate you, give yourself a break and let it go.

Remember, the basic concept with the idea of movement as a way to nourish your body is this … take every opportunity to move more, doing activities that you actually like, ideally on a daily basis. It's as simple as that. Don't make it more complicated. And do not forget that everything counts.

❧ SELF-CARE DARE ❧
SCHEDULE YOUR MOVEMENT ACTIVITIES

Your next step is to "schedule" your movement activities on your calendar. Note the type of activity and the actual timeslot that you will commit to for the coming week. Then, do this each week. I recommend a specific day of the week where you do this type of planning. Sunday evenings are usually a good time to do some planning. While I do not prescribe movement plans, I do recommend that you get more intentional about natural movement in your life while also planning to get thirty minutes of intentional movement activity into each day as a starting point. We'll talk more later in the book about setting intentions and goals, which will help you further explore how much movement is meaningful for you.

CHAPTER FIFTEEN

←— THE POWER OF PLAY —»

"You can discover more about a person in an hour of play,
than in one year of conversation." ~ Plato

I'd like to add to this quote by saying that the person you discover through play may just be yourself. In order to live a life committed to true sustainable self-care practices, we must tap into more powerful internal resources. Participating in various forms of PLAY is one of those resources. When was the last time you truly *played* for the sake of playing?

Play is not just essential for kids; it can be an important source of relaxation and stimulation for adults as well. Playing with your romantic partner, co-workers, pets, friends, and children is a sure (and fun) way to fuel your imagination, creativity, problem-solving abilities, and improve your mental health. Actively playing with your kids will not only improve your own mood and wellbeing, it will make your kids smarter, better adjusted, and less stressed too.

In our modern, hectic lives, many of us focus so heavily on work and family commitments that we never seem to have time for pure fun. Somewhere between childhood and adulthood, most of us stopped playing. When we do carve out leisure time, we're more likely to zone out in front of the TV or computer than engage in fun, rejuvenating play. Developing your self-care practices offers a huge opportunity to buy yourself some self-care time and redirect it so you can tap into the power of play. Enjoying activities where we have no external goals or milestones to reach connects us back to our center, the root of who we are, and offers us glimpses of our souls. There does not need to be any point to the activity beyond having fun and enjoying yourself. And you get tremendous health benefits to boot. What a concept!

Play shifts our minds into a more expansive arena, which allows us to connect more deeply with others in a space where we can then entertain diverse perspectives, relax rigid beliefs, and tap into our own inner creative center. Playing together for the fun of it brings joy, vitality, and resilience to your life and to your relationships. It's the creative outlet where bold discoveries and aha! moments are born. Stress release, problem solving, and creative solutions live here. Play allows us to truly enjoy the efforts we've put into being committed to our truest needs. It helps us to stay in grace and gratitude for our lives.

You can play on your own or with a pet, but for even greater benefits, play should involve at least one other person, away from the sensory overload of electronic gadgets. As is listed at helpguide.org, here's a deeper look at the benefits of play:

- ✔ **Stress Relief.** Play is fun and can trigger the release of endorphins, the body's natural feel-good chemicals. Endorphins promote an overall sense of wellbeing and can even temporarily relieve pain.

- ✔ **Improve Brain Function.** Playing chess, completing puzzles, or pursuing other fun activities that challenge the brain can help prevent memory problems and improve brain function. The social interaction of playing with family and friends can also help ward off stress and depression.

- ✔ **Stimulate the Mind and Boost Creativity.** Young children often learn best when they are playing—and that principle applies to adults as well. You'll learn a new task better when it's fun and you're in a relaxed and playful mood. Play can also stimulate your imagination, helping you adapt and problem solve.

- ✔ **Improve Relationships and Connection to Others.** Sharing laughter and fun can foster empathy, compassion, trust, and intimacy with others. Play doesn't have to be a specific activity; it can also be a state of mind. Developing a playful nature can help you loosen up in stressful situations, break the ice with strangers, make new friends, and form new business relationships.

- ✔ **Keep You Feeling Young and Energetic.** In the words of George Bernard Shaw, "We don't stop playing because we grow old; we grow old because we stop playing." Playing can boost your energy and vitality and even improve your resistance to disease, helping you feel your best.

Play might look like simply goofing off with friends, sharing jokes with a coworker, throwing a Frisbee on the beach, doing a jigsaw puzzle, drawing with sidewalk chalk, using crayons to color in a coloring book, dressing up at Halloween with your kids, building a snowman in the yard, playing fetch with a dog, participating in a game of charades at a party, or going for a bike ride with your spouse with no destination in mind. Remember to supercharge your playtime by disconnecting from the sensory-overload of electronic gadgets. By giving yourself permission to play with the joyful abandon of childhood, you can reap the many benefits outlined above.

I challenge you to remain open to the opportunities to reclaim your inner child by setting aside quality playtime in your life on a regular basis. Surround yourself with playful people. They'll help keep things light and will help support your efforts to play and have fun. Be spontaneous, set aside your inhibitions, and try something fun, something you haven't done since you were a kid perhaps. Here are some additional *play* ideas to consider:

- ✔ Host a regular game night with friends
- ✔ Go bowling, play pool or miniature golf
- ✔ Sing karaoke
- ✔ Fly a kite
- ✔ Build a Lego structure

✔   Play hide and seek with a child

✔   Build a sandcastle

Secret Tip: Find ways to combine play with movement. Now, that's a time maximizer!

❧ SELF-CARE DARE ❧
ADDING MORE PLAY

How can you add more play into your life? List some ways. When will you do it? How often? Add your thoughts to your self-care journal.

CHAPTER SIXTEEN
« — THE NEED FOR SLEEP —»

Sleep, like nutrition and physical activity, is a critical determinant of overall health and wellbeing. Good quality, regular sleep plays an essential role in your self-care practices. You already know that sleep makes you feel better, but its importance goes way beyond just boosting your mood or banishing under-eye circles. Sleeping well is absolutely essential to your physical health and emotional wellbeing. It also improves concentration, memory, and has tremendous restorative qualities. Nighttime sleep helps the body mend cell damage that occurred during the day and can refresh the immune system, which helps prevent disease and infection. It's one of the most fundamental things I address with every client, since it seems no one I've ever worked with has shown up with healthy sleeping habits. Poor sleep quality is a chronic issue.

How you feel during your waking hours hinges greatly on how well you sleep. The cure for sleep difficulties can often be found in your daily routine. Your sleep schedule, bedtime habits, and day-to-day lifestyle choices can make an enormous difference to the quality of your nightly rest.

The following tips will help you optimize your sleep so you can be productive, mentally sharp, emotionally balanced, and full of energy all day long.

THE SECRET TO GETTING GOOD SLEEP EVERY NIGHT

Well-planned strategies are essential to deep, restorative sleep you can count on night after night. By learning to avoid common enemies of sleep and trying out a variety of healthy sleep-promoting techniques, you can discover your personal prescription for a good night's rest. The secret, as it is for any other self-care practice, is to experiment. What works for some might not work as well for others. It is important to find the sleep strategies that work best for YOU. While sleep requirements vary slightly from person to person, most healthy adults need at least seven to nine hours of sleep each night to function at their best. Keep your personal sleep target in that range as well.

Set a sleep schedule. Getting on a sleep schedule is one of the most important strategies for achieving good sleep. If you keep regular sleep hours, going to bed and getting up at the same time each day, you will feel much more refreshed and energized than if you sleep the same number of hours at different times. Consistency is vitally important here. If you are getting enough sleep, you should wake up naturally without an alarm. If you find that you need an alarm to wake you on time, you may need to set an earlier bedtime. When is your ideal bedtime and wakeup time? Also, try not to break this routine on weekends, when it may be tempting to stay up late and sleep in.

Develop a toolbox of relaxing bedtime rituals. One of the key ingredients to getting a consistent good night's sleep is establishing a relaxing bedtime ritual. This is especially important if you find it difficult to shut down for the day. Slowing down with a specific bedtime routine can promote the relaxation you need to wind down. If you make a consistent effort to relax and unwind before bed, you will sleep easier and more deeply. A peaceful bedtime routine sends a powerful signal to your brain that it's time to wind down and let go of the day's stresses.

Every small effort you make to calm your body and mind will add quality to your sleep time and help you create an environment that will allow you to relax and ease into a sleepy state.

Here are some ideas:

- ✔ Read a book or magazine by a soft light
- ✔ Take a warm bath
- ✔ Listen to soft, calming music
- ✔ Do some easy stretches
- ✔ Wind down with a favorite hobby
- ✔ Listen to books on tape
- ✔ Sip on a warm cup of herbal tea
- ✔ Try some deep breathing techniques
- ✔ Lower the lights to induce production of melatonin, the hormone that helps you fall, and stay, asleep

Make your bedroom a sleep sanctuary. Make your bed as inviting as possible with cozy, comfortable bedding and pillows. If your mattress is old and tired, consider an upgrade. Keep noise down. If you can't avoid or eliminate noise from barking dogs, loud neighbors, city traffic, or other people in your household, try masking it with a fan, recordings of soothing sounds, or white noise. Earplugs may also help. Keep your room cool. The temperature of your bedroom also affects sleep. Most people sleep best in a slightly cool room (around 65° F) with adequate ventilation. A bedroom that is too hot or too cold can interfere with quality sleep. And last, but certainly not least, reserve your bed for sleeping and sex only. Identifying that space with anything else can impede your ability to relax.

Unwind early. If you know you need to get to bed by 10:00 p.m., it won't do your sleep efforts any good to be moving at lightning speed until 9:59 pm. It's important to shut down the television, computer, smart devices, or other high-stimulus activities at least two hours before sleep. Allow your mind to shift gears from work mode to rest mode.

Eat and drink with sleep in mind. Your body is a machine that stays fired up as long as you give it food and drink to metabolize. Avoid big meals at night. Eat dinner as early as possible in the evening and avoid heavy foods or any food you know could upset your system later. Limit your alcohol intake. It may help you fall asleep faster, but it reduces the quality of sleep. You might also wake up in the middle of the night with a dry mouth and headache. Not desirable. Cut down on caffeine. Some people can have sleep problems from caffeine they drank ten hours earlier! Switch to water or herbal tea after lunch.

Hydrate, but not too late. If you drink lots of tea, juice, or water into the evening there's a good chance you'll be up in the middle of the night for a bathroom break. The goal is to avoid sleep disruption.

Take smart naps. Napping is a great tool to make up for lost sleep. If you need to make up for a few lost hours, opt for a daytime nap rather than sleeping in late. This strategy allows you to pay off your sleep debt without disturbing your natural sleep-wake rhythm, which often backfires in insomnia and can throw you off for days. If insomnia is a problem for you, consider eliminating napping. If you must nap, do it in the early afternoon and limit it to thirty minutes.

Clear your head. A quick journaling session at the end of the day is a great way to clear your head of worrying thoughts or lingering to-dos. Before lights out, allow yourself five minutes to write down all your stressors, which could include things like work challenges, conflicts with others, or financial concerns. Also, write down one or two steps you can take toward resolving the stress. Before you put the journal away, write down at least three things you are grateful for. All of this helps to put your stress to rest.

Use calming scents. Specific aromatherapy oils can have a calming and sedative effect when inhaled. You can put them on your skin (wrists, bottoms of feet, temples) or place them in a diffuser so the scent spreads throughout your room as you fall asleep. Breathe in the relaxing fragrance as you drift into dreamland. The diffuser will continue to provide scented relaxation as you sleep.

Ways to get back to sleep. It's normal to wake briefly during the night. A good sleeper won't even remember it. But if you're waking up during the night and having trouble falling back asleep, the secret is to stay out of your head. The key to getting back to sleep is continuing to cue your body for sleep, so remain in bed in a relaxed position. Hard as it may be, try not to stress over the fact that you're awake or unable to fall asleep again, because that very stress and anxiety encourages your body to stay awake. A good way to stay out of your head is to focus on the feelings and sensations in your body or to practice breathing exercises. Take a breath in, then breathe out slowly as you say or think the sound, "Ahhh." Take another breath and repeat. Make relaxation your goal, not sleep. Remind yourself that although it is not a replacement for sleep; rest and relaxation still rejuvenate your body.

If you have been awake for more than fifteen minutes, try getting out of bed and doing a quiet, non-stimulating activity, such as reading a book. Keep the lights dim so you do not cue your body clock that it is time to wake up. Also avoid screens of any kind— computers, TV, cell phones, tablets —as the type of light they emit is stimulating to the brain. A light snack or herbal tea might help relax you, but be careful not to eat so much that your body begins to expect a meal at that time of the day.

If you wake during the night feeling anxious about something, make a brief note of it on paper and postpone thinking about it until the next day when you are fresh and the issue will be easier to resolve. Similarly, if a brainstorm or great idea is keeping you awake, make a note of it on paper and fall back to sleep knowing you'll be much more productive and creative after a good night's rest.

There is a vast amount of research on the subject of creating restful sleep patterns. If you are seriously sleep deprived, it may be time to address it with additional homework. Make it a priority to research this topic further and discover ways to honor yourself by getting the sleep you need. If none of these strategies work and you are not getting enough sleep, it's most likely time to get serious and see a professional to have a sleep study done. The quality of your life literally depends on it.

❧ SELF-CARE DARE ❧
THE ROLE OF SLEEP

In what new ways will you honor the role of sleep in your life? Be specific. What new actions will you take? Add your thoughts to your self-care journal.

part 4

« NOURISHING YOUR MIND » AND SOUL

If you nurture your mind, body, and soul, your
time will expand. You will gain a new perspective
that will allow you to accomplish much more.
~ Brian Koslow

CHAPTER SEVENTEEN
←— CULTIVATING A HEALTHY MIND AND SOUL —→

A healthy mind and soul is absolutely crucial to your overall wellbeing. You must nourish all pillars of self-care (mind, body, and soul) to truly nurture your entire life. All aspects of your being are interconnected. Have you ever heard of the notion that we are spiritual beings having a human experience? I remember when I first heard that, and it instantly shifted my belief system around the immense power of nurturing my soul. If you seek true body nourishment and want to address health and wellness by being more mindful about your thoughts and actions relating to your physical body, it is highly unlikely that you will get permanent results unless you address body, mind, and soul as a single unit. You will gain strength in all three areas by focusing on them as a whole. For instance, using the power of your thoughts to resist your body's cravings for comfort food helps you satisfy body-related goals. It's an interconnected system of power and grace.

Often in pursuing what we believe to be our hopes and dreams, we power through without giving a lot of thought to what we are actually doing. We lose touch with our true inner needs. If we ignore it long enough, that disconnection asserts itself, perhaps with a vague sense of unease. We may feel that something is not quite right in our lives, but we can't put our finger on just what it is. We may seem to have everything we should expect in life, yet we are somehow not happy or satisfied. There is an emptiness. This is our soul seeking our attention, prompting us to address the missing links and to reconnect with our true needs.

As with nourishing your body, you need a balanced and conscientious way to feed your mind and soul. Like real food, our mind and soul require a wide variety of spiritual nutrients for a healthy, successful, and rewarding life steeped in a commitment to self-care. This requires an appropriate mix of both stillness and action. You need periods of sleep, rest, and relaxation to recharge your physical strength and your mental faculties. If you don't allow for recuperation time, you will get worn out, physically and mentally. In this section, we'll cover activities that will be useful in developing your own bio-individual approach to nourishing and flourishing your mind and soul.

As with everything in this book, the material isn't intended to be all-inclusive of every possible tool. I will share a collection of what I deem to be the most powerful ways to begin nurturing your mind and soul in new ways. They are a collection of the ways in which I have helped my own life and the lives of my clients, and I know they are extremely impactful. My hope is that the content we do cover will inspire you to think about ways to build your own path towards mental and spiritual growth. It's in your hands to find what connects and inspires you the most and take action from there.

THE UPSIDE TO DOWNTIME

"We live in a culture that perpetuates the belief that when we have a lot going on and a lot of excitement, we're really alive," says Anne LeClaire, author of *Listening Below the Noise: A Meditation on the Practice of Silence.* "In truth, we are really alive when we can be at peace within our own skin." Stillness and downtime are the secret to connecting with that peace.

Practices dedicated to nourishing your mind and soul *must* include periods of downtime and stillness that allow for inner silence and quiet reflection. You won't hear me say "must" or "should" very often, but there it is, a must. Through these practices you become more intuitive about your truest needs, learning to listen to the inner voice that comes from your soul and inner wisdom. It may seem counterintuitive to take time out when your to-do list is a mile long, but the fact is that consciously doing nothing can actually make you feel healthier, more energetic, and more alive. It can also help you enjoy life more. And yes, in case any of my fellow ambitious, driven, overachievers are wondering, you'll be more productive as well. There's a reason why sabbaticals exist; to help us restore and fill up again. Stillness also includes moments of mindful connection with the inputs we receive from the external world, like taking in the wonderment of a beautiful natural landscape or listening to a song that stirs your spirit. These sources of inspiration can create quiet contemplation and connection that refresh our soul.

Even for those with the best intentions to live balanced lives, the modern world demands that we are almost always connected and productive, and this can drain us emotionally, spiritually, and physically. Intentional downtime creates more open space in our lives to do more and be more. It resets the crazy and refuels our lives with what really matters. If you are truly committed to self-care, downtime is absolutely essential and *sacred*. This is time for you to do nothing in particular but spend some time with yourself. It's an opportunity to hit the personal pause button in our lives and literally (and figuratively) take deep breaths. It's also the place where epiphanies are born. And don't we all need more of those?

LEARNING TO REST

Surprisingly, most of us need to learn how to rest. It's not a natural skill we possess, unless we have already been practicing. It's a skill we need to learn in order to make it a priority. The more we can integrate periods of downtime into our daily lives, the bigger the payoff will be. The amount of downtime you need is very personal and may vary from time to time. Your individual needs depend on what is going on in your life at a given moment or period of time. During more tranquil periods, perhaps you won't need as much downtime, but during periods of crisis, more downtime might be required. The important thing is to make it intentional and treat it as sacred.

Take a crystal clear look at your life to see where you have or have not allowed space for downtime, then explore ways that you can introduce more into your life. Keep in mind that when you begin restful practices, you may at first find them uncomfortable. If this is a new practice for you, you just might bump up against emotional turbulence. Resist the temptation to flee the turbulence and jump into busy mode again. Allow yourself to stop, acknowledge what you feel, then breath and move through it, knowing that this is incredibly beneficial to your soul.

WAYS TO PRACTICE DOWNTIME

One incredibly awesome way to practice honoring downtime is by participating in restorative yoga. In case you've never tried it, it is the quintessential stress-reducing yoga practice. In restorative yoga, you use more props than in other forms of yoga, including blocks, cushions, and blankets. This helps to support the body while it's being held in various yoga poses for longer periods of time. Restorative yoga also stimulates the part of our nervous system that invokes a relaxation response, which results in lowering heart rate and blood pressure, relaxing muscles, and creating softer, more rhythmic breathing. It is absolutely worth a try. It could become your new healthy downtime addiction.

Another idea is to take a nap. Taking a nap is a powerful way to recharge. "When you take a nap, you're not just doing something for yourself, you're making a statement to the world that there is something that is at least equally important and productive as working, and that is doing nothing," says Rubin Naiman, PhD, a sleep specialist and clinical assistant professor of medicine at the University of Arizona's Center for Integrated Medicine. Being a nap queen, I high-five this statement and highly recommend that you take more purposeful naps.

In addition, here are some other downtime ideas. Remember the idea here is to enjoy this time *alone*.

- ✓ Conscious breathing and counting your breaths for a few minutes
- ✓ Drinking a cup of tea
- ✓ Reading something inspirational
- ✓ Taking a bath
- ✓ Writing in your journal
- ✓ Meditating (we'll talk more about this in a minute)

It's helpful to set a specific time for rest and put it on your calendar. We absolutely need to put boundaries around that time so we can claim it for ourselves.

ๆ SELF-CARE DARE ๆ
CULTIVATING A STRONGER CONNECTION

Select one new idea from this chapter to try in the next week in an effort to begin to cultivate a stronger connection to your mind and soul. Which one will you choose?

CHAPTER EIGHTEEN
« CREATING PURPOSEFUL PAUSE »

Mind and soul numbing . . . that's basically what we're doing to ourselves when we *constantly* have the TV on in every room at home or the radio on in the car or the music cranking in our ears during every workout. We are always blowing our brains up with stimulation. We need to turn the noise off, enter into silence more often, and give ourselves an opportunity to "detox" from media and technology. Silence and stillness is investing in purposeful pause. It is the place of soul-connecting incubation. If this is a new practice to you, at first it might feel like nothing much is happening when you get still, but if you create a space for sacred silence and stillness, your life will experience profound beneficial shifts. It's inevitable. Silence and stillness practices are the most powerful ways that I know to manage chaos and stress and to re-connect with your inner wisdom.

Sitting in silence, meditating, and breathing techniques are some of the most popular practices.

MINDFULNESS AND MEDITATION

"There's simply no way we're going to attune to the rhythms of life if we don't slow down and create some space for silence."
Matthew Kelly, *Rhythms of Life*

Mostly, we live and act on automatic pilot, dutifully adhering to unconscious habits, letting our mind wander wherever it desires. While this can be a necessary way to live at times—such as when we are coping with something particularly challenging and simply need to be in survivor mode—a more intentional and powerful way to tend to our self-care needs is by being more connected to what we are actually doing by being *mindful*. Taking a mindful approach to your self-care and your life simply means taking note and being more aware of where you are in the present moment, identifying with the pleasures of this present moment, and perhaps what you need to change so you can experience it more profoundly. It's about being completely attentive to the present and living in the now. Mindfulness connects you with your environment and creates awareness of where you are in it and how you engage with it. It's a deep level of attentiveness that opens you up to experience the real essence of things with your senses. You can truly enjoy the sight of colors and the smell of scents in nature. You can take in the feeling of rain falling on your body or a breeze blowing across your face. You can savor the lingering taste of food. Mindfulness revitalizes, invigorates, and energizes you by connecting you fully with what you are doing in the moment. As the self-care goddess you are becoming, it is essential that you spend some time finding ways to connect more mindfully in your life. Mindfulness is fundamental to staying in tune with all other aspects of self-care as well.

One of the very best ways I know to create more mindfulness is through regular meditation. Our minds wander about restlessly, aimlessly, always on the move. Our passing thoughts jump continuously from past memories to present problems to future fantasies, never sitting still. We worry, we plan, we go over our regrets, we relive our victories, we relive our shame, and replay the highlights and lowlights of our day. We live in fast forward and rewind, rarely in play, and never, it would seem, in pause.

Meditation allows you to pause, find your inner vision and light, and truly connect with it and use it in your daily life. It can also help you to release past conditioning and begin to choose new paths that will serve you better for going forward in your life. You can find your happy place in meditation, because it allows you to get grounded and centered, which carries you through your day in a mindful way. It also is an incredible way to begin to detox the mental clutter that no longer serves you.

My personal experience with meditation has absolutely changed my life. I had suffered with extremely debilitating anxiety and panic attacks on a daily basis for almost two years before I began a regular meditation practice. Quite honestly, I wish I had tried it much, much sooner. The panic attacks always hit me as soon as I awoke in the morning, which was generally very early, between 3:00 and 4:00 a.m. The stress, anxiety, panic, and heart palpitations would kick in immediately. It felt like I couldn't breathe, like someone was squeezing my heart and crushing my chest. I always tried to talk myself out of these attacks and rationalize my way through them, saying things to myself like, "Whatever I'm worried about isn't real," or "For crap sake, Shelley, this is ridiculous. Just stop it." Well, none of that self-talk worked. The challenge for me was that much of the time I couldn't even identify what I was actually concerned about. It was like the panic attacks had a mind of their own. Unfortunately, they never failed to show up, every single morning of my life.

Sometimes I could get myself calm enough to go back to sleep or at least to rest for a little longer, but most of the time I ended up getting out of bed and beginning my day. Several people suggested that I use medication to help, but I refused. I have been on lots of medications in my life, and still take some for my migraines, but I was absolutely *not interested* in taking anything more.

I don't recall exactly what prompted me to want to try meditation, but my life changed *significantly* because of it. I thought that perhaps meditating in the wee hours of the morning when I woke with a panic attack could help me relax again and get back to sleep. I started small, using an app on my phone that provided guided meditations, which progressively built up from ten minutes to twenty minutes at a time. I committed to doing that daily for a few months. Then, I learned about a different way to meditate that included a structured process to carry my mind through various thought patterns, including connection, gratitude, forgiveness, visualization, and daily intention, always ending with a blessing. I listened to the guided version until I memorized the basic framework, then I put it to my own music and took myself through the sequence.

Meditating in this way was a much bigger time investment.

It could take me up to an hour to go through the entire sequence, but that's when my panic and anxiety started to wane and my life began to take on an entirely new tone. I noticed that my mind was much more at ease and I was able to stay present, focused, and calm at times when normally I'd be in stress mode. I was able to see things differently and find my power center to stay grounded for longer periods during the day. I was doing a lot of other personal development work at the time, too, but there was something about meditating that took things to a whole new level.

I did the structured sequence meditation for almost a year, then I got turned on to the guided meditations offered by Deepak Chopra and Oprah Winfrey through the Chopra Center. I've purchased and completed every single one that they offer and I absolutely love them. I have now been meditating every single morning, right when I wake up, for nearly two years, and my life has been forever changed. I can't even imagine starting my day without it. I don't even think you could pay me to not meditate. It is part of the keys to helping me dismount into an amazing day each day. I very rarely experience panic or anxiety attacks anymore, and if one does show up as a result of my zealous ambitiousness, I now am able to reconnect with what is real very quickly. I cannot say enough good things about how meditation can be a powerful tool in your self-care toolkit. I wish every single person on earth could discover it and make it a part of their life.

If you want to give it a shot, and I obviously suggest that you do, here are some ideas to begin.

MEDITATION 101

Choose a convenient time and a quiet, comfortable place for your meditation practice. Consider what items you need to remove or have around you to support a feeling of calm and serenity. Take action to create your meditation sanctuary by setting up a space to support you. There are special pillows that allow you to meditate seated comfortably on the ground, or maybe you prefer to sit on a chair. If you would like to burn a candle or incense, have them ready in your sanctuary. There are no rules; what you use to create your special sanctuary is totally up to you. I tend to be a lazy meditator, so I lie in bed with pillows to prop up my legs. Also, I meditate with my earbuds in, so I can listen to soothing music or a guided meditation without disrupting my husband when he is home. I bought a nice set of earbuds as homage to my practice, and I use them every single day.

Make sure you won't be interrupted. Let the members of your household know when and where you will be meditating and for how long. Set boundaries around this time so you and others will honor your space. Or better yet, invite curious family members to join you!

Set an intention. Intention is a powerful tool for transformation. Before sitting down to meditate, ask yourself, "What would I like to manifest in my life today?" or "What would my inner wisdom like me to know?"

While there are some meditation practices that foster very specific ways to practice, ultimately there is no right or wrong way to meditate. Simply make the commitment and try it out. You can meditate by sitting in silence and counting your breaths, even for just one minute, or you can do a more structured guided meditation.

It's your choice. Then, go for it. Know that your mind will wander throughout meditation and it's okay. The moment you recognize that you are focused on something besides meditation, release the thought and gently bring your mind back to your meditation. Don't make the fact that your mind wanders a big deal. Do this process as often as you need during meditation. Ultimately, the best way to approach the practice of meditation is to simply trust your journey and know that your meditations are unfolding just as they should be. Never judge it.

Additionally, forms of moving meditation are also extremely beneficial and include practices like yoga, tai chi, and Qigong. In these forms, the physical changes in the body cause the relaxation. The release of endorphins makes you feel good and reduces your stress levels. Check these out if you feel inspired to do so!

ᴇ SELF-CARE DARE ᴇ
BEGIN A MEDITATION PRACTICE

How will you begin a meditation practice? What can you commit to, to get started? One minute a day, five minutes a day? As with the other self-care activities we've discussed, schedule a time on your calendar. For meditation, I highly encourage you to start small and be consistent so you can create a micro-habit. If you begin with five minutes a day, try it every single day at the same time each day for at least two weeks so you can truly evaluate it. Then, expand as you are ready.

CHAPTER NINETEEN
«— GRATITUDE —»

Gratitude shifts our awareness, changing our approach to ourselves, to others, and to the world. Living in gratitude means being thankful, counting your blessings, noticing simple pleasures, and acknowledging everything—and I mean everything—that you receive, even experiences that are burdens. It means learning to live your life not only *as if*, but actually knowing and feeling that everything *is* a miracle. It means constantly being aware of how much you've been given. Being a gracious receiver is also a big part of living in gratitude, which can be quite a challenge for some of us. In fact, people have written entire books about how to receive graciously.

Gratitude adjusts your focus from what your life lacks to the abundance that is already present. Giving thanks for all things, even being able to shift those things that you might normally perceive as "negative" into "feedback and learning" makes people happier and more resilient. It's far easier to feel grateful when everything's rockin' along in life. The trick is to center ourselves in gratitude when things go sideways. It's a lot easier to do that by practicing gratitude day in and day out—creating a *disposition* of gratitude, where we can build up some gratitude stamina and are fully prepared when the really challenging times come—as they inevitably will! It helps us bounce back from challenging circumstances more quickly, strengthens relationships, reduces stress, and improves overall health and wellbeing.

It's also really important to stay centered in the knowledge that it's during our challenging times when we tend to grow the most. They offer us the opportunity to powerfully clarify our values and live them with integrity. When faced with a challenge, we can move quickly into gratitude by getting curious and asking ourselves questions such as "What's good about this?" "What can I learn from this?" and "How can I benefit from this?"

Quite simply, there is nothing more life-changing and ultimately self-loving and nurturing than living in gratitude in your life right now and in every single experience that you will have from this very moment forward. Gratitude changes your relationship with life from an attitude of rejecting and defending to acceptance and appreciation, which is a much more connected way to live.

"If the only prayer you say in your life is 'thank you,' that would suffice."
~ Meister Eckhart

When was the last time you really stopped to take note of the things you are grateful for? It could be anything that brings you true joy, even something as simple as a great cup of tea. To help with this practice, here are some ways to get you into gratitude mode on a regular basis, ideally on a daily basis.

Say thanks. Send a thank-you message to someone who did something special for you. If someone goes out of their way in any way, shape, or form, identify it, internalize that blessing, and openly express your gratitude. Share with them how much you appreciate their act of kindness. To step up your gratitude game—handwrite a note to them and stick it in the mail. For people or circumstances that warrant it, write a longer letter, detailing how their act of generosity benefited you, and email or snail mail it. Better yet, schedule some time with them and tell them in person. Read your letter to them if the situation moves you to do so. Just express, express, express.

Keep a gratitude journal. Every morning (or evening), write down three to five things you are grateful for. They can be simple things, or big things. It can be something that happened recently or in the past. The key is that they're different every day. Think about what happened that was surprisingly fun, exciting, or laugh-out-loud funny. What made you feel good or proud or connected to someone else? Doing it at night right before you sleep can be a helpful bedtime ritual to get you calm and centered for restorative sleep.

Use visual cues. Write notes or collect objects that elicit feelings or reminders of gratitude and put them in different places so you see them throughout the day to help set your gratitude habit. In your bathroom, on a nightstand, on the fridge, kitchen cabinet, on your work desk, in your car—wherever you spend time and will see those items and get triggered to stay in gratitude.

Meditate on gratitude. Conduct a daily self-guided gratitude-based meditation. Get yourself settled into stillness and review a mental list of all the things you are grateful for. Maybe set a timer too so you stay in gratitude for a specified period of time.

Set up a gratitude challenge … and commit to it. Set up a start and end date. I recommend at least twenty-one days to create the momentum of a new habit. Do something each day that is a reflection of gratitude. Wear a special symbol, like a charm bracelet or an inspirational necklace. Print and post a quote or write on your bathroom mirror with sharpie. Set an alarm twice per day to remind you to have a "gratitude moment"— anything that reminds you to stop and be in gratitude. Practice a daily ritual during that time to reflect and give thanks for all the little and big things in your life that bring you joy. You can also do a gratitude journal during your challenge. Take note to disrupt the voices that show up to complain, judge, criticize, or gossip with a powerful pause, then reset that voice to shift into gratitude.

Gratitude should not be just a reaction to getting what you want, but an all-the-time way of being, the kind where you notice the little things and where you constantly look for the good even in unpleasant situations. Today, start bringing gratitude to your experiences, instead of waiting for a positive experience in order to feel grateful. Appreciating whatever shows up for you recalibrates your vibration, helping you to find the beauty of what is versus what you are hoping for. It helps you get truly, authentically present in your life. If you make the choice to find the gift in every situation, whether easy or difficult, you start to become your own miracle worker. You will see and experience life and everything it has to offer from a place of transformative non-judgment. Gratitude moves us from fear into expansion, and literally nothing will be able to stop you.

‿ SELF-CARE DARE ‿
FOCUS ON GRATITUDE

How will you begin a focus on gratitude? Journal at least one way that you can take action to add more gratitude goodness into your life.

CHAPTER TWENTY
« GENUINE CONNECTION AND COMMUNITY »

Nothing is more satisfying in life than connecting—truly and genuinely connecting with another person or group of people. We absolutely need genuine connections to be truly happy and fulfilled. It's your sisterhood, your tribe; where you regularly connect with your people to share ideas, get inspired, get outside of your own head, challenge your existing (dare I say limited) belief structures, and add value to each other's lives in profound ways. And, by the way, we all have a tribe. Sharing with your "sisters" or in your tribe is where self-development practices can be developed and where growth happens. It doesn't even matter how you connect, whether it be in person, by phone, or perhaps through a favorite social media outlet.

For me, it's even a way to learn about what's going on in the world. By choice, I don't watch TV or keep up with the mainstream media, because it adds little nourishing value to my life, so I get most of my worldly information by hearing it from others. I can take in the new knowledge and gain insights about people's perspectives at the same time. A genius connection play if I do say so myself.

Connection also feeds a strong sense of belonging, which is self-care nourishment at its most fundamental level. It's where we explore acceptance of ourselves and others, and it can be a source of solace when we are coping with particularly challenging life struggles. A sense of belonging to a greater community improves our motivation, health, and happiness. When we truly feel our connection to others, we can intuitively know that we are not alone. There is tremendous comfort in that knowledge.

All the money in the world, and the best job, and all the material possessions one might accumulate won't matter much if we live in total solitude and have no genuine human connections to share with. Relationships give us a sense of belonging in the group and an almost therapeutic support system. We learn from others' experiences and insights, and we learn together by pursuing new experiences alongside those in our tribe. The interactive exchanges with other human beings add richness to our lives.

If we can allow ourselves to be exactly who we are, genuine connection can be a safe haven where we can be seen, heard, and valued, which then can ultimately allow us to see our own true selves even more clearly, honoring each layer of growth and expansion. Genuine relationships create psychological space and safety so that we can explore and learn. When we feel safe and supported, we are able to explore our world and our potential for growth.

Through genuine connection, we are able to thrive. It is such an important element of self-care and life that it's actually part of our survival mechanism. It is a primary need. Think about a baby. If the baby didn't come into the world with the ability to connect with and entice their parents or caretakers to care for them, they would not survive. All humans need other people in order to be well and thrive. We feel better simply by being around other people. Close relationships bring a happiness factor that doesn't exist without them, whether that connection rests with just one other person or an entire group. When we work together in groups, we can accomplish more than as individuals. Truly, by being connected we are stronger.

One of the missing links is that we usually skim the surface with others, staying in small talk and choosing to protect ourselves, to maintain our poise, and to not allow ourselves to be seen. We socialize online, but that can actually keep us at a "safe" distance. We work with people, but often that's task-oriented rather than an invitation to deeper connection. We interact with family and friends, but when we are busy, distracted, and overwhelmed by life, those connections might stay on the surface level as well. We may feel too busy to truly be with and "see" other people. The fact remains that we have a human need for this kind of connection, and there's no doubt that it makes us happier.

SPECIFIC WAYS THAT CONNECTION BENEFITS US

It boosts creativity. Working in solitude can be a great way to create, and having some time for solitude is important for reflecting on ideas, but having a healthy and authentic discussion with someone is extremely important for expanding ideas. When you get together with a friend, or talk over something with a family member, you will inevitably walk away with several new or reinvigorated ideas to explore.

It creates opportunities. When you eliminate networking, simply for networking's sake, and shift into a mode of true connection with someone, new opportunities for collaboration and creation emerge that weren't there before.

Belonging to a group or community gives us a sense of identity. It helps us understand who we are and allows us to feel part of something larger than ourselves. And more often than not, people are happier when they are with other people rather than when they are alone. In addition, people with strong social connections have less stress-related health problems, lower risk of mental illness, and faster recovery from trauma or illness. Friends and family can also encourage and support us in healthy lifestyle habits, such as nutrition and movement.

You might feel that genuine connections are hard to find but "finding" them isn't the answer. You have to make it a point to be intentional and create them. In a world full of amazing and interesting people, there is nothing more beautiful than knowing how to form healthy relationships and establish deeper connections with those around us.

There is no dispute that connecting with other humans makes you happier. And when you're happier, you're more enjoyable to be around. The feedback loop continues: you engage more with your tribe, increase personal happiness, are more fun to engage with, continue to increase personal happiness, engage more, and so on. Yet, many adults struggle to make and maintain connections amidst the "go go go" of modern life. Because, as adults, there are much fewer built-in "friendship development opportunities" (aka "school," "sports," and "the neighborhood"), it's worth exploring what you can do if you'd like to cultivate connection in your existing tribe or if you're interested in branching out to discover a new tribe of friends and relationships.

FOSTERING GENUINE CONNECTIONS

You can't force a connection to be what you want it to be. Many people make this mistake. They try to create a connection with someone who doesn't want it, or hope the person responds in a certain way, or want the other person to be something they're not, and so on. This can only lead to disappointment. I've discovered that the key to an unforced, genuine connection is openness.

FIRST and foremost, make time for your most important relationships. Identify the primary, most important relationships in your life. It might be your spouse and kids, or other family members. It could be a best friend or small group of friends that are like chosen family. Or maybe it's a boyfriend or partner. No matter what else is happening in your life, it's critical to make time each day for these primary relationships—even if that time is spent taking a walk or sitting down for a meal together and talking, really talking and really listening. If a relationship is important, create time in your life to nurture it. This could also extend to a small circle of close friends that you might not see every day, or even every week. Schedule time to check in with them or be with them in person. Then, be your true self when you do get to spend time together. True connection shows up when you are being your truest version of you.

Reach out! And not just when it's a special occasion.
You have technology at your fingertips. Use it. Message someone
to say hello and tell the person that you are thinking of them. Use
video-chat to actually see the face and hear the voice of your friend
who lives far away. As a kid, you went to see if your neighbor could
come out and play, not because it was a "special occasion" but
because any old day was a good day to play. As adults, we often start
compartmentalizing our social time into "special occasion" territory
only. Celebrating someone's engagement or a major holiday become
the reasons we get together instead of getting together simply because
it's a good day to have a casual get-together. Connecting can happen
over a big evening out with a bunch of friends all dressed up, but it
also can happen for thirty minutes in the middle of a Sunday over a
quick cup of tea at your house.

Be open to random connections. Set an intention to stay
open to the possibilities of new connections. While you obviously
won't have time to entertain every new possibility that comes your
way, stay open to feel out which people jive with your true self. Stay
in curiosity. Be open and maintain a sense of wonder about who
someone else really is. Stay out of judgment and share yourself openly.
You never know what can happen from that place of openness. What
might look seemingly random could be the connection of a lifetime.
Even if it's just a "moment" with someone else, share it with as much
openness as you can muster. You could be an absolute light for
someone else and vice versa.

Be open to who someone else truly is. Try to notice your
expectations of the other person and let them go. Don't pigeon-hole
the person or try to make them someone they're not. Simply explore

who they are without knowing what you'll find. Stay in curiosity. You'll find the real them this way, and it's almost always far better than finding what you hoped to find. If it's not, you already know how to set boundaries around the situation so that you stay true to what you need.

Socialize without an end game in mind other than "to get to know them better." People can sense a true desire to connect. Be genuine with your intentions. Engage without an agenda, without focusing on how they could help you or your career. Along with that comes the important reminder that you shouldn't default to an assumption that someone else has ulterior motives in starting a conversation with you either. Make no assumptions. Part of building your tribe and feeling a sense of connection and community is being open enough to allow others into your world.

Ask questions and listen to the answers. There is an art to good conversation. It begins with a genuine interest to hear the other person. Be curious. Show interest. Ask follow-up questions. It's not about proving how much you know, being right, or sharing only about you. Conversation is a dance you enter into where sometimes one partner leads, and in due time, the other partner leads, and at some points no one is leading at all. Be bold enough to ask courageous questions, maybe something like, "What's the biggest mistake you've made this year?" Then, engage fully in their answer. This is a very quick way to move past small talk and into the beginning stages of genuine connection.

Be open about yourself. Often we try to present a certain side of ourselves, depending on who else is in the room or the dynamics of a particular situation. We try to come across in a very particular way, maybe as competent, knowledgeable, interesting, accomplished, funny, or savvy. Often, those are masks and misrepresent who we really are. Why bother trying to connect with someone when we're just going to give them a false identity? It doesn't serve you. It doesn't allow you to expand and honor who you really are. While it might feel like a risk, it is better to open yourself up and show the real you. This is scary. It means being vulnerable, which takes a huge amount of courage, especially when you can't be sure of an outcome. But it's totally worth it. When you become vulnerable, it might feel like a risk, but you also get much, much more out of the experience. You get trust from the other person. You get a deeper connection. You get a better friendship. They open up more, too. And when you've tried this a few times, you will realize there isn't much risk at all. Everything you learn and gain from the experience adds tremendous value to your life and growth.

And finally . . . if you're connecting in person, put your phone away. This one needs no explanation. Just do it. Put your phone away, or at least put it on silent or vibrate mode. Pay attention to the present moment that is happening with the person, or people, you are with.

There are numerous types of friendship. And those friendships may form with the most unlikely of people. Why? Because both parties show up to that friendship without the pretense of anything beyond, "Hey, you're cool, let's spend time together." Practice this perspective and get connected!

❧ SELF-CARE DARE ❧
CREATING CONNECTIONS

Answer the following questions related to the connections in your life:

- ✔ How are you fostering connection and community in your life?
- ✔ What new activities might you participate in to get more "connected"?
- ✔ When will you make time to include those new activities in your schedule?

Add your thoughts to your self-care journal and spend a moment reflecting on where you can add more connection goodness to your life.

CHAPTER TWENTY-ONE

← SELF-EXPRESSION AND ACTS OF SERVICE →

Just as much as it is crucial to have moments of stillness, silence, to be in gratitude, and experience connection, you also need periods of spiritually-centered action to nourish your mind and soul. These may be acts of self-expression or works of service to others.

Healthy self-expression is essential to nourish your soul. The ability to live a life centered around self-care nourishment is a determining factor in how well you're able to express. Self-expression exercises the muscles of your inner creative energy, which is an incredibly powerful way to reflect inward as well.

All of us are capable of being creative, through our work or through activities like writing, performing music, drawing, painting, decorating, gardening, or other pastimes and hobbies. Life is filled with opportunities to express the creative power of our soul, strengthening the connection with our inner wisdom and source of higher consciousness. Beyond that, as an innate part of our human existence, we're here to make a difference. We do that through love and legacy, to make the world a better place for our loved ones, and ourselves, and for those who will be influenced by our presence in their lives. Believe it or not, all of this is impacted by our wellness, because being in a state of great health through self-care makes us able to more fully express our human potential at all levels: body, mind, and soul.

Total self-care means that physically your body's cells, tissues, organs, and systems are fully functioning; mentally you are cognitive, your emotional and social functions are healthy; and you are growing spiritually, assured of your personal worth, trusting in your wellbeing, with a sense of meaning and purpose underpinning your life. You and all living things have an innate intelligence. Your life is an expression of this intelligence through your body, mind, and soul. The quality, and ultimately the worth, of your life depends on your ability to express this intelligence to your fullest potential.

It is generally well known that bottling up your emotions is unhealthy. In fact, prolonged inability to release anger or frustration can lead to physical illness, and not just minor conditions like headaches, nausea, or skin rashes. Chronic failure to express your emotions can lead to much more serious, even life-threatening illness. Releasing toxic emotional blockages is as important as cleansing chemical toxins from your body. Toxic spiritual blockages are of even greater concern. Feelings that drain your spirit include loss of self-esteem, a feeling that life is meaningless, and beliefs that your situation is hopeless, you are worthless, and there's no point in carrying on. Such feelings lie at the root of depression, despair, and spiritual malaise.

People facing hopelessness or despair may lose their will to live, succumbing to illness and even death. In many cases, this hopelessness is learned based on past conditioning. It is critical that we recognize these patterns and rise above this type of learned helplessness, because resignation causes harmful biological effects like suppressing or shutting down the immune system. The purpose of learning to nourish your soul is to minimize the risk that you will succumb to spiritual sickness. One of the key strategies you can adopt is to find ways in which you can express yourself. Strategies like this are actually spiritual practices, although they may not seem to be. They are aimed essentially at reaching deep within yourself, beyond emotions, mood, and self-image, and expressing and developing the creativity and intuition that lies in those deep places. Effectively, such practices aim at connecting you with and nourishing your soul.

Here are four such practices that involve expressing yourself through your work, writing, pastimes, and art.

SELF-EXPRESSION

Your Work. Chances are you spend a great deal of your time doing the work that helps pay the bills. It's a heaping big chunk of most of our lives. In fact, on average in America, people will work from age eighteen to sixty-five, a total of forty-seven years, and spend about 109,980 hours working during that time. At some stages of life, you may spend more time working than being engaged in most other life activities, including sleeping. Given just how much emphasis we put on our work lives, it should go without saying that we *should love* what we do. The ideal work life is one that nourishes us. If it doesn't provide that, it's time to take a good, hard look at other options.

You will be more successful in life, and happier and healthier, if you love your work. This is true no matter what your trade, business, or profession. What matters most is being able to truly connect with the personal meaning and significance in your work, so that it feels more like a calling, or a life mission, than merely a job. If, instead, your working life brings you frustration rather than fulfillment, you may be suffering from work stress, which is one of the biggest causes of stress in a person's life. Consider changing your job and doing something you love. If that is truly not an option for you at the present time, reach deep inside and see if you can find a new attitude about your work; a new approach that will give it greater meaning. In fact, many jobs offer greater scope for service, contribution, and the ability to make a difference than we may realize.

Most of the clients I have worked with to date struggle in this area. It takes time to explore and feel out other options. Create space to start thinking about what needs to change to get you into a more nourishing work situation in your life. Life is too short to do work that constantly drains you. It's cliché, but it's true.

As I explored ways to continue to make financial contributions to our family that connected to my soul, it's amazing what has evolved. Several years ago, I set a strong intention to be emotionally, spiritually, and mentally connected to my work. Most days, what I do doesn't even feel like work. It feels like a blessing to wake up and be in a creative zone where I am nurtured beyond anything I could have imagined previously. I am extremely passionate about the work I do, and it absolutely serves as my life mission. Now, don't get me wrong, there are definitely things about my work that challenge me to the core, but being able to do work that I love changes my attitude about even nitty gritty tasks, such as bookkeeping, for instance. My work gives me the opportunity to impact lives in ways that feel significant and meaningful for me.

And I didn't just get lucky—I created this experience. I keep a piece of art above my office chair that reminds me of how important it is to do meaningful work that I love. "When You Do What You Love, Everything Else Falls Into Place." Yes indeed!

Writing. Expressing our deepest feelings in a journal helps us connect better with our inner selves. This inner self knows far more about us than the less than authentic versions of ourselves that show up to live out our lives most days. Confiding in a secret journal is like confessing to an understanding friend or therapist; and there's great healing in that space. When you unburden yourself of your innermost fears, guilt, regrets, and fantasies, it gives you the freedom to let go of them, releasing emotional and spiritual blockages at the same time. When you write down your aspirations and dreams for the future, you sharpen your vision and goals, and set your unconscious mind to attract the energies you need in order to live your dreams.

As we've already discussed, another excellent writing exercise is to keep a gratitude journal. This practice will increase your overall happiness level, boost your health, improve your lifestyle habits, and increase your optimism, which are essential foundations for nurturing your soul. Each day, record in your journal at least three things you're grateful for that day. Reflect and be thankful for a variety of things each day. It will keep your mind focused on the positive aspects of your life and can be a secret weapon in shifting your mindset if you are experiencing something particularly challenging. Having a horrible day? Get into gratitude. It truly changes everything. You can be grateful for a great conversation with a friend, a delicious meal, a special note from a child, a great walk in nature, colorful flowers, or making progress on a big project. Identify and connect with what has positively impacted you in any way. Living in gratitude is a powerful way to nourish your soul and feed your wellbeing.

You may also think of other ideas for writing projects that help you nurture your soul. You might research and write your family history, write your own life story, or create poetry. Doing the work of understanding and expressing your innermost knowledge, beliefs, and feelings about a subject will help you get used to connecting with your inner self. This is how you develop your intuition and nourish your soul.

Pastimes and Hobbies. It's quite common to plop down in front of the TV at the end of a long day as a way to unwind. Many people play computer games, aimlessly surf the net for celebrity gossip, or get immersed in social media for hours on end. Too much of this mindless type of passive relaxation numbs the mind. It may feel like a way to "check out," but it actually saps your spirit, starving it of nourishing stimulus. If you take an honest look at how many hours per day or week you spend on these types of activities, there may be an incredible opportunity to buy yourself some time to spend on more nourishing activities that will actually help you grow in all of the areas we've already covered related to your self-care. I encourage you to use your spare time in more energizing, intentional, and purposeful ways. Spend it in pastimes that nourish your soul; activities that nurture your spiritual life and make you feel good about yourself in the process.

Make up a list of things you have an interest in or are passionate about. Your list may include activities like gardening, landscaping, DIY projects, or interior decorating, to name just a few. You may prefer to take up an activity such as dancing, yoga, or tai chi, or a sport such as swimming. There are endless possibilities. Activities pursued mindfully and creatively offer many benefits, both internal and external.

Art. Learning to express yourself through art is a powerful way to nourish your soul. And just know that when it comes to artistic pursuits, pure talent is overrated. Simply spending time in passion and devotion is the magic ingredient. The bonus is that while you build your skill, you're doing something you love and having fun. You do not have to be a Rembrandt or a Michelangelo. We all have some level of natural ability to express ourselves artistically. Doing something with it is what matters, not winning art contests or impressing people.

There is literally something for everyone. You can draw with pencils, ink, or crayons. They even have amazing adult coloring books now that are proven to reduce stress simply by coloring in them. Or you can paint with watercolors, acrylics, or oils. You can carve, sculpt, or cross-stitch. You may like knitting or sewing, creating personal fashions, or producing homemade gifts for family, friends, or a favorite charity. If you love music, learn to play an instrument or join a choir and sing. It doesn't matter how good you are—that's beside the point. Please yourself with your determination and progress.

ACTS OF SERVICE

Giving of ourselves in various capacities can actually be an ultimate self-nourishing act, helping us connect with our inner caregiver. Generosity and altruism are a part of human nature. We are born with a natural desire to help others. In fact, as humans evolved, survival depended more on cooperation than on competition. In the face of danger and hardship, those who protected their families and other members of their tribe were more likely to maintain their support network and be helped in return. They had a greater chance of passing on their genes.

But there's more to it than that. Our feelings of altruism go beyond reciprocal support within family and tribe. We feel concern and compassion for complete strangers, not just family. True, family comes first; however, the plight of the poor, the suffering of the sick, and the desperation of the downtrodden tug at our heartstrings, even when those in need are strangers. Charity absolutely begins at home, but it certainly doesn't end there.

Any time you show kindness to a total stranger or give your time freely, you're responding to something deeper than a need to survive. Think about it for a minute. Some people sacrifice their lives to save the life of another or spend their lifetime in pursuit of a cause greater than themselves. There are also philanthropists who give away entire fortunes to alleviate the struggles of complete strangers. Such actions clearly aren't conducted for personal survival. Giving, as it turns out, really does make us feel good. People who are kind and generous to others, and who serve meaningful causes that transcend their self-interest, are in fact happier and healthier and lead more fulfilling and satisfying lives. Generosity empowers us, builds our self-esteem, strengthens our sense of meaning and purpose, and helps us feel that our lives have value.

Acts of service do not need to be grandiose gestures in order to count. They don't have to be your work or your life mission. Acts of service can simply be a new awareness and mindfulness about ways that you can add more generosity into your life. In living my life as a wife and mom, my acts of service are involved mostly around my family, especially the kids. By choosing to view tasks as acts of service—such as driving kids to school and extracurricular activities, doing laundry, helping with homework, making dinner—that change in perspective shifts my entire belief system around those activities.

Outside of family-related acts, you can do things for others that require little or no effort. Gestures such as opening the door for someone, or driving someone to the airport, or helping neighbors with tasks like collecting their mail, watering plants, or watching their house when they are out of town are all small offerings that help others in big ways. There are infinite ways to do little things that don't feel overwhelming but add tremendous value to your own life simply by being in service.

ᶜᵉ SELF-CARE DARE ᵉᶜ
DO SOMETHING DIFFERENT

What ideas from the self-expression and service pool of thoughts inspire you to do something different in your own life? Write them in your self-care journal in addition to any actions steps you want to take.

part 5

←← SETTING YOURSELF UP →→
FOR INEVITABLE SUCCESS

*Success is nothing more than a few simple disciplines
practiced every day.*
~ Jim Rohn

CHAPTER TWENTY-TWO
‹‹— THE PRICELESS NEXT STEP —››

REALIZING GOALS THROUGH INTENTIONS

We've covered some serious ground, looking at ways you can begin to focus and address powerful energies around nourishing and flourishing your self-care habits. We've looked at ideas to make these habits a way of life, building Team YOU in the process. If you recall, Team YOU is the support system you design for yourself with your own thought processes and by building up valuable resources, people, programs, and processes that support your desired commitment to self-care habits. If you've been working through the Self-Care Dares and exercises, you've actually been building Team YOU all along the way.

We've also talked about the need to deliberately choose to live in a way that serves you, as well as multiple ways you can address your fundamental needs related to your body, mind, and soul. Considering what you've read up to this point, it's time to identify what is most significant and begin to shape ways to take inspired action steps to make self-care a reality in your life.

Setting practical self-care intentions and goals is the priceless next step, but I'm not going to lie, it can feel daunting. This is where people can get hung up. However, with the work we've done up to this point, we've intentionally paved the way to make this process much easier. From a nuts and bolts perspective, to achieve a new self-care practice, it's essential to spend some time envisioning a future outcome that you desire and then plan. From there, you apply sacred discipline in order to create new habits that will help you achieve your goals. Through the Self-Care Dares and exercises, you've already spent some time visualizing and connecting with your actual needs. Moving into intention and goal setting will help you organize your time and energy, which will provide direction for your commitment to self-care as a way of living. Committing to specific goals will absolutely assist you in your efforts, but the process must start with intentions.

Goals involve visualizing an imagined future and are not concerned with what is happening to you in the present moment. With goals, the future is always the focus. Are you going to reach the goal? Did it allow you to achieve the happiness you expected? Then, what's next? Setting intentions is quite different from setting goals. It is not oriented toward a future outcome. Instead, it is a path or practice that is focused on how you are "being" in the present moment. Your attention is on the "now" in the constantly changing flow of life and allows you the space to be in that flow. You set your intentions based on understanding what matters most to you, and you make a commitment to align your actions with your inner values.

By being in touch with and acting from your true intentions, you become more effective in reaching your goals than when you act from wants and insecurities.

If you are truly connected to your WHY around self-care, you will then be open to your truest intentions and your goals will unfold naturally. However, your intentions are always the foundation for your goals. As you gain clarity and insight through reflection, your ability to act from your intentions blossoms. It's a continuous practice; an ever-renewing process. You don't just set your intentions and then forget about them. You live them every single day. Goals help you to stay in continuous forward motion and be a productive person, but being grounded in intention is what provides integrity and unity in your life. It is the fuel that sparks your goals.

Through cultivating intention, you learn to make wise goals and then work toward achieving them without getting stuck in attachment to a specific outcome. Only by being grounded in your intentions can you reconnect with yourself during times of emotional storms that cause you to lose touch with yourself. This "remembering" is a blessing, because it provides a sense of meaning in your life that is independent of whether you achieve certain goals or not. The question to reflect on becomes much more about whether or not the actions that you took honored your innermost values rather than the actual outcome. And there's always progress and growth in that space.

Intention is what provides you with self-respect and peace of mind, even when you may not be living up to every goal you set for yourself. It is an empty exercise to measure the success of your life by only looking at what you achieve or do not achieve. The far more empowering philosophy is to prioritize how aligned you are with your deepest values. Goals are ever-changing. Intentions are more rooted and grounded and are your source of true inner meaning. Yet, goals are necessary to propel you forward.

Because the concepts of intentions and goals are deep, let's explore each one further. So, get ready to roll up your sleeves and dig in.

SETTING INTENTIONS

What's your big vision for your overall wellbeing? That's a mighty big question to consider, but it's also crucial to explore. It's time to get connected and get real with yourself. This is where you get to truly honor your whole being.

Intention is the starting point of every new adventure. Everything that happens in your life begins with intention. When you decide to celebrate, to learn something new, or even to give yourself a break, you start with intention. Intentions assist you in taking greater control of your life. In case you haven't spent much time considering the concept of intention, let's define it. A working definition of intention is, "to have in mind a purpose or plan, to direct the mind, to aim." If we lack intention, we can stray without meaning or direction in our lives. With it, we can create the experiences we truly desire. Your absolute desires around what you want to manifest in your self-care focused way of life begin with intention. Intentions can relate to something specific or be more like a quality, such as having the intention to be more relaxed or connected. People set intentions related to all kinds of dreams. Their intentions may be connected to their desire to get married or have children, to get a job or make a career change, to write a book, travel more, lose weight, or even to move to a foreign country. When you set an intention and then set goals to act on it, you demonstrate your commitment to your intention. That's when amazing life-transforming things occur. Additionally, intentions can give us fortitude for dealing with tough times because they can provide us with focus and a beacon of hope. Powerful intentions can even help you maintain composure, sanity, and a good sense of humor.

SETTING INTENTIONS AROUND SELF-CARE

"The quieter you become, the more you can hear."
~ Ram Dass

By setting an intention, you make it clear to yourself, and anyone you choose to share it with, that you are focused and committed to a particular dream or activity. This sets desires and collective energies into motion.

Listed below is the very basic intention-setting process. In this chapter, we will be working directly with Step 1, where you will clarify your intentions. Then Steps 2 through 4 subtly and naturally get addressed. You can use this structure for any intentions you want to set in your life. For our purposes, however, we will be specifically looking at your intentions around your regular, daily self-care habits.

The basic four-step intention-setting process is called CSSA, which stands for Clarify, Share, Start, and Acknowledge.

1. **Clarify**. This is the first step in the intention-setting process. It helps you get clear about the TOTAL self-care

experience you want to create, addressing mind, body, and soul. You get a chance to dive into the ultimate vision for your life and how you want to live it from the foundation of self-care first, as a launching pad for everything else you do. In a moment, you will go through a visualization exercise, to dream a little, and then write down what shows up. The complete exercise is explained below. The idea with this step is to get as detailed as you can about how you want to *feel* as a result of your new way of living.

The remainder of the four-step process is outlined below. While we won't go specifically into each one of these steps, they do get addressed as you move through the remainder of the book materials. I want to share them with you here as a framework, so you can see the entire intention-setting process and connect with the follow-through that comes after the first step.

2. **Share**. Share your intention with someone who will supportively hold you accountable to take action. Who is on Team YOU and can play that role? Identify them and then ask if they would be willing to listen and participate in your journey. You might even inspire them to join you, and then you can help each other stay accountable.
3. **Start**. Start taking action today (even if it's a tiny, micro-step) to demonstrate your commitment to your intention. What step can you take right now in this moment to follow through on the intentions you set?
4. **Acknowledge**. Take time to acknowledge that you did

what you said you would do. Celebrate your movement into action and then take the next step toward honoring your intention.

Now, it's your turn to do some intention-setting. We'll be focusing on Step 1 of the process described above—CLARIFY.

To set yourself up to complete this exercise, first read through the entire exercise described below. There are questions to reflect on as you get still (and close your eyes) so you can focus your mind on your intentions. I want you to be aware of what to reflect on while your eyes are closed, so you won't have to peek. Then, when you re-open your eyes, you'll be writing down your reflections.

To help create the environment for stillness and reflection, play a slow, meditative song to help you relax and connect to your inner voice. I've also heard this voice referred to as inner wisdom, which is a term I really love. This exercise is meant to amplify the voice of your inner wisdom. Be sure to have your journal and a pen ready to go as well.

Ready. Set. Here we go.

It's time to get quiet and still. Sit upright, with your feet on the ground. Close your eyes and take eight to ten slow, calming breaths to ground yourself and prepare to connect with your intentions around your powerful self-care journey.

After you get relaxed, begin to reflect on what experiences you would like to have in your ideal life of self-care. Is it more relaxation? Less stress? More energy? More connection? More sleep? More time to nurture your mental activities? A stronger commitment to a spiritual practice? Doing more yoga? Eating more in alignment with the way you want to feel? Moving more? What has shown up for you as you've read thus far? What new inspirations struck you?

The idea is to deeply connect with what you want to create that serves you best. Reflect and visualize what that looks like and feels like as you sit in stillness. Picture it in as much detail as possible. Once you feel that you've clearly painted that picture in your mind, open your eyes and write down everything you heard from your inner wisdom. Do not judge. Just write. Don't stress out if you couldn't hear anything your inner voice was saying. Simply write down anything that showed up for you. This helps set the stage for answering the next questions, which will tap into what you visualized and help you set to your intentions. Read through the questions, then write your answers in your journal.

- Ѵ WHY is this focus on self-care important to you? Write down anything that comes to mind, in no particular order or format. Just get it out of your head and onto paper.
- Ѵ Where are the current gaps in your self-care approach? What would you like to change? What intention could you set to meet those needs? For instance, maybe you'd like to experience less stress. To help with that, you can set an intention to spend more time in play and meditation. Don't concern yourself with anything beyond what the general actions might be at this point. We are not focusing on specific ways yet. Our efforts here are on simple reflections and initial intentions.

Clarifying your intentions gives them power to be brought to life. I believe that each of us knows exactly what we need to do to nurture our self-care, but life can get so noisy and "busy" that we become deaf to our own inner voice. Hopefully, your inner voice got to be heard through this exercise.

Whatever you wrote in your journal for the CLARITY part of the CSSA intention-setting process is now your compass and launching pad for setting practical goals that will drive your daily behavior and habits. Sit with what you've written and allow it to sink in. You can even reflect back on this exercise and do it again and again as you grow and as new self-care needs arise. Solid, heartfelt intentions carve the path toward your tangible goals. This is where you start to align your WHY with your intentions, which will ultimately fuel your actual daily behaviors that will lead you to achieving your goals.

❧ SELF-CARE DARE ❧
INTENTION SETTING

Complete the intention-setting work and reflection activities outlined in this chapter. Create time in the next few days to focus on this work.

CHAPTER TWENTY-THREE

← FROM INTENTIONS TO PRACTICAL GOALS →

All of the work you've done up to this point is building a foundation for your current and ongoing self-care. Energized by the Self-Care Dares and exercises you've completed from the previous chapters, I expect that you are now intimately connected to your WHY and your INTENTIONS for wanting to live in alignment with your commitment to self-care. Now, it's time to get some goals on paper.

Without a doubt, you will find greater success in putting your self-care plan into action if you set and work toward specific goals. It allows you to be captain of your own ship and chart a course, as opposed to sending a ship off to sea with no captain and no plan. That would end in disaster. A plan with solid goals is necessary. Many people find that by first setting definite goals and then breaking each goal into small, manageable steps, change feels less overwhelming and more achievable. When setting goals, keep them realistic and achievable.

We will first focus on goals, then create a plan, monitor progress, and adjust accordingly to ultimately propel you and keep you moving forward. This is how your new habits will form.

Things to consider when setting goals, whether they are related to self-care or otherwise, are control factors, simplicity, pace, and timing. We'll cover each of them here.

Control Factor. Make sure it is something that YOU control and is not dependent on anyone else to be accomplished.

Simplicity. Do not overwhelm yourself. Keep it SIMPLE. Begin with your #1 non-negotiable self-care need and move on to other priority needs from there as your time, energy, and desires allow. My #1 non-negotiable self-care need happens to be personal time, with meditation coming in as a very close second. I know that if I don't get enough consistent personal time, my life begins to unravel big time, and it's not pretty for me or anyone else who is influenced by my presence. For me, personal time means time spent completely alone, doing absolutely whatever it is that I want to do, with no expectations, no timeline, and no agenda. I might take a bath, take a nap, read a book, sit and stare at the birds outside, write in my journal, or create a special music playlist. Because this is so essential to my personal self-care, I always have a goal related to creating time in my schedule each week to honor personal time. The day, timing, and activity look different each week, depending on what else is going on, but it's always a priority. For many of my clients, getting more high quality, rejuvenating sleep is a #1 non-negotiable self-care habit they create goals around. Perhaps that one resonates with you as well.

Pace. Trying to do too much too fast can dilute your energy and ultimately land you right back at the starting point, or worse. That is not motivating. It's defeating. I have a dear friend who shares a lot of similar self-care philosophies as I do. She shared a story with me recently that really drives home the idea of being mindful of pace when someone sets goals.

She had spent a solid six months studying for and taking exams to become a CPA. She sat for countless hours each day for six months straight in pursuit of that goal. It was incredibly intense, since most people cover the same material in eighteen months, yet for various timing reasons, she chose to do it in six. Sitting and studying was her full-time job for that period of time. She did not participate in any physical activity during this time whatsoever, and when all was said and done, she had gained some weight and was feeling extremely drained and frustrated. She felt she'd been forced to neglect her health and wellbeing while she studied in order to focus every single second of every single day studying and testing. Once the studying and testing was over, and she felt the tremendous relief of having passed the exams with flying colors, she was ready to get back into sync with a lifestyle that was more health supportive.

Participating in regular physical activity in her life was one of those ways. As she was preparing to get back into the swing of health-centered living, she saw a flyer for an upcoming Ironman triathlon race and got inspired. She thought that perhaps this was exactly what she needed to get motivated to move. She had never done anything like it before. An Ironman is a *serious* race. It consists of a 2.4-mile (3.86 km) swim, a 112-mile (180.25 km) bicycle ride, and a 26.2-mile (42.2 km) marathon run, raced in that order and without a break. It takes an average athlete about thirteen hours to complete and obviously includes a multi-disciplinary training approach with an emphasis on swimming, biking, and running.

When she shared with me what she intended to do, I gasped (inside) and laughed nervously (out loud), thinking that perhaps all of that focused CPA studying had inhibited her cognitive abilities in other areas. Who goes from sitting for six straight months, never having trained for or competed in an Ironman before, to jumping into the intensity of training for that race? Then, I thought, *Well, of all of the people I know, she just might be able to pull this off.* We joked that doing an Ironman after sitting for six straight months was clearly the obvious next step, right?

She was fired up and began her training right away. Guess how long it lasted? Two weeks. She got so overwhelmed with the multi-disciplinary training protocols and the need for her training to be like a part-time job that she freaked out and went right back to where she started, but not without beating herself up a bit before she landed back at ground zero.

The point here is that you don't need to go from the couch to preparing for an Ironman event. That's not practical for most of us. Start with self-care practices that are small and do-able, at a pace that may feel like a little stretch, but not so over-the-top that you will feel even more stress. Then, add in more self-care practices as you accomplish the ones you previously identified. It will give you a much greater sense of success, and it all adds up to better self-care habits and an ongoing way of living. The little wins that you get along the way provide great fuel for your future activities.

My friend ended up adjusting her self-care goals to drinking more water each day and going for regular walks to help with her energy and body-shaping intentions. She is and has been able to stay on track with doing each of those regularly, and I celebrate her for modifying to a more practical approach where she can get some "wins" into the mix before jetting off into Ironman-land.

Timing. For our purposes, we will address your top self-care goals to be accomplished in three different time periods: one month, three months, and six months.

Now it's your turn to get into goal-setting mode. Read through the entire exercise before you begin, to familiarize yourself with the process and the layout of the goal-setting sheet first. You can use a blank sheet of paper for this exercise or you can go to *www.selfcare101book.com/bonus* to download a blank worksheet to fill in.

Review the goal sheet presented here, and if using your own sheet of paper, duplicate the framework first.

Date: _____

SACRED SELF-CARE GOALS
Building Team ME

MY WHY:

In this area, note YOUR biggest whys captured throughout this book. What did you identify as the fundamental reason why you want to commit to a different way of living around your self-care needs?

MY INTENTIONS:

In this area, note your intentions from the exercise in the previous chapter. What intensions did you identify as your starting point?

BODY	MIND AND SOUL
One Month:	One Month:
Three Months:	Three Months:
Six Months:	Six Months:

Now, check back with your self-care journal and reflect on all the areas we have explored and the various ways to take action on nourishing and flourishing your body, mind, and soul. What are your new non-negotiable self-care needs and what small goals can you establish to honor them? We are focusing on baby steps here. What one or two inspired actions can you accomplish in each of the timeframes? Identify body-related goals that can be accomplished in each of the timeframes on the goal sheet. One month, three months, and six months. Also, identify mind and soul-related goals that you'd like to accomplish in one month, three months, and six months from now.

The idea is not to overwhelm yourself, but to stretch yourself in ways that you know you can accomplish. I encourage you to get outside of your comfort zone. That's where growth and progress live. You are dedicated to both of those values, right?

As a handy reference tool, here are the areas we've covered. You may not have specific goals in each of these areas. The idea is only to include actions that resonate for YOU.

NOURISHING YOUR BODY

- Ⅴ Loving your body
- Ⅴ Addressing nagging ailments
- Ⅴ Feeding your body (including ideas for mindful meal planning)
- Ⅴ Movement
- Ⅴ The power of play
- Ⅴ The need for sleep

NOURISHING YOUR MIND AND SOUL

- ✔ Cultivating a healthy mind and soul (including downtime)
- ✔ Creating purposeful pause (befriending silence and stillness)
- ✔ Living in gratitude
- ✔ Genuine connection and community
- ✔ Self-expression and acts of service

After creating your goals, take a moment to celebrate yourself for being where you are at this moment. For connecting with your why, setting intentions, and documenting inspired goals to support your whys and intentions. That's a big step! There is tremendous power in writing these things down. It brings clarity to your purpose, which will propel you forward much faster. It also frees up room in your mind, removing unnecessary clutter so you can connect with forward momentum, and finally, research tells us that you are far, far more likely to accomplish things that you document. So, let's celebrate that. Go YOU!

The critical next step is to save what you have created and post it in plain sight. If you want to solidify the process even more, share it with anyone who will listen to what you are up to. If you have others in your household, share it with them. The goals that you included on your sheet will shape your daily activities and help you stay on track to accomplish them in the specified periods of time. What you've written can get you into inspired action and intentional, deliberate practice mode—if you allow it to do so.

Now, this is when the rubber meets the road, so to speak. Get out your calendar and commit to when and how you will take action on your goals. Write down your inspired action steps and block out the time on your calendar. This is how self-care supporting habits are born. If there is anything in particular that could motivate you to stay on track—such as a picture, a vision board, a particular event, or a feeling—connect with that and make it a part of your daily life. Also, tap into how you've been successful in the past. Why did that work? What pulled you away from that activity? What can you change to create a different experience now? Tap into whatever works to inspire you and get your activities scheduled. Actually making the mental connection to schedule the activity and see it on your calendar makes it far more likely you will accomplish it.

The invitation is for you to give up low-commitment-living and step up your game. Give yourself permission and choose to commit consciously to honor your self-care needs and to make them a natural part of your life. Set up habits that can run on autopilot. What are you taking a stand for? Hold that vision and deflect the noise and static that might try to take you off course. Stay connected with people and circumstances that ignite and inspire you and be open to new sources that emerge. It's never too late to start, but START now. Don't wait until your body, mind, and life are screaming at you to do something different. Make self-care a priority now, while the stakes are still low.

I often get asked about discipline and willpower. I think Matthew Kelly says it best in his book, *Perfectly Yourself,* when he talks about the correlation between happiness and discipline. People ask how much discipline they should exert, and his answer, "Well, how happy do you want to be?" It takes about that much discipline. And you are absolutely worth it.

‹e› SELF-CARE DARE ‹e›
GOAL PLANNING

Complete the goal-planning sheet that is part of this chapter. Sit back, review it, and celebrate yourself.

CHAPTER TWENTY-FOUR

«— WHAT IS INEVITABLE SUCCESS? —»

We all have twenty-four hours in each day. How you specifically use that time is a total expression of where self-care falls in the spectrum of your life. We've covered a lot of different ways to prepare yourself for making self-care a priority. I know, however, that it's not realistic to tend to every single one at the same time. We do not need to be superheroes. Nobody wins that game. Recall that the main idea is to find the self-care activities that YOU best connect with and prioritize your focus on them. You simply need a starting point and a focus. Things will adjust as you move through this journey. Leave room for exploration and adjustment as you continue to learn what works for you, and as your needs change.

While truly honoring your self-care needs does not require a grin-and-bear-it or a do-or-die approach, it does require a certain amount of sacred discipline to uphold it as a priority in your life. Simply knowing that real self-care and self-love blesses the lives of not only yourself but of everyone in your sphere of influence is often not enough to take continued inspired action to honor your self-care needs. Based on everything we've covered so far, you have now created a basic framework for meeting your self-care needs, but what I want to cover in this chapter are the special strategies for making sure that you set yourself up for inevitable success; ensuring that you actually do what you intend to do, without a lot of stops and starts.

The concept of inevitable success is simply identifying any limiting factors or barriers that might prevent you from achieving what you want to achieve and then brainstorming ways to remove those obstacles. It brings a new awareness into the circumstance and allows you to see things differently, with a sense of possibility rather than defeat.

In my coaching practice, we talk a great deal about "inevitable success" as a powerful way to choose parameters that help my clients stay on track with their self-care intentions and goals. Preparing for inevitable success allows them to take ownership in a refreshing way, so they can remain focused on their priorities without excuses, loss of momentum, or having to start over. Essentially, what they do is reflect on what is truly needed in order to have success with a given self-care goal and then take action to put that need in place. It might be something like having a courageous conversation with a family member to let them know what they are up to on their specific self-care path and sincerely asking for support (and giving them very specific guidelines about how to do that). Or it could be buying a new pair of athletic shoes or shoe inserts so their feet don't hurt when they go for a walk. This process takes away any underlying potential barriers, removing excuses and breathing new, focused energy into the goal.

For instance, if you feel you can't eat in a more nourishing way because you don't know how to cook, ask yourself how you can solve this issue so you don't use it as a limiting factor. The truth is, you don't have to know how to cook or even want to cook to upgrade your eating. There are always creative work-arounds to accomplish that desire. Bust through the barriers and keep momentum going each day, each week, each month, and each and every year until the place you land in the not-so-distant future is somewhere far more dedicated to self-care than where you are starting from.

In working with my self-care coaching clients, I've heard about and helped navigate the way through a great deal of barriers. Sometimes they are obvious barriers that can be identified and addressed easily. At other times, the barriers don't start to surface until we've been working together for several months. Some of the less obvious barriers turn out to be small issues, like no longer enjoying the playlist of music they have on their music player so they don't want to go for walks anymore. Something like this can be fixed easily with some accountability around scheduling enough time to add new zest to the playlist. Easy. At other times, issues can be bigger. It could be that a client is frustrated with not feeling like they have enough time to focus on self-care. This is a big one and it remains the #1 obstacle for most women. In that case, we always begin with some inner work about self-worth and look for ways to make self-care a priority. There are also additional strategies that can help in re-shaping their circumstances so they actually can make self-care their priority, and we look at those.

While what will help you set yourself up for inevitable success is deeply personal, here are a few ideas to get the juices going. These are ones that have helped my clients tremendously. See what connects for you and start thinking about how you can address them in your life. There is an opportunity at the end of this chapter for you to capture ideas that are specific to you and your circumstances.

Releasing the "BUSY" Mindset and Time Creation. As I mentioned, by far, one of the biggest obstacles I hear about on a regular basis is women feeling that they do not have enough time in their already jam-packed lives to focus on self-care. Yet, most of them come to me when they've had enough and are so broken down that they know they need to do something in order to feel better about their bodies and their lives. Have you heard the phrase, "Nothing changes if nothing changes"? That applies to all aspects of life, and definitely to making changes in honoring your body, mind, and soul in new and nourishing ways. We all have the same amount of hours in a day, but it's the way we perceive those hours and then use them that matter.

I used to have an extremely unhealthy obsession with time. I was really busy—beyond busy. Life was busy. Everyone I knew was busy. We loved to say that word repeatedly to anyone who would listen—busy, busy, busy. It was the canned response I said and heard every time someone asked how it was going. I was so busy, in fact, that I virtually never actually sat down to eat a meal. I would stand up to eat so I could race off at any moment, which seems absolutely crazy to me now. It always felt overwhelming when someone would ask me to do something on top of what I had already planned for myself. There was no time for that. I was sleeping an average of four hours a night, for months in a row, just so I could be awake longer and be in constant productivity mode. It even bothered me that other people could sleep when there was so much to do all the time. Needless to say, I was a stressed out, panic-ridden mess. This was one piece of the collection of experiences that led to the big meltdown I described in the beginning of this book.

Once I finally began to peel back the layers of my story as it related to time, I discovered that "busy" was simply a mindset. When we keep repeating how busy we are, it's not just the people we're talking to who hear that. Our brains hear it, too. To some degree, I think we're overwhelmed because we're telling ourselves we are. I have done a lot of recovery in this area. It didn't change overnight, but I was able to release some serious garbage around my ideas with time, and it allowed me to make space for the fundamental self-care needs that would begin to change my entire life, including my ability to sleep for longer periods of time, which brought body nourishment to an entirely new level.

I can almost hear some of you saying, "I am busy and it's just not the right time to tend to my self-care needs." Or, "Shelley, you can't possibly understand MY life and what is going on for me … self-care just isn't possible." Perhaps you think you'll take a look at self-care later when you have more time. In actuality, the "right time" is going to be the moment you release the busy mindset and DECIDE that self-care is a priority. There is no magical act of fate that will somehow provide a clearing in your schedule to let you make self-care a priority. You have to give yourself permission and choose to make time to work on it.

I also want to challenge you to begin at this moment to avoid referring to how hectic, busy, or overwhelmed you are and definitely refrain from using the word "busy." Just hearing it now makes me shudder. I've now chosen more empowering and motivating words like "productive" or "full." When someone asks me how things are going, I now respond in a way that honors and celebrates all of the activity I have going on. I might say, "I'm rockin' some super productivity right now. I have lots of exciting projects I am working on." That's *far more* empowering than, "Well, you know, it's busy as always." It's amazing how impactful just deciding to view things differently and using more inspiring words can be. When you can truly move past this, you will be rewarded with a new perception on time and miraculously will have much more time to focus on mapping out a nourishing and flourishing self-care plan for yourself to maintain focus on Team YOU.

Another incredibly powerful way to add more actual hours into your life is by being mindful of mindlessness. How much time do you spend watching TV? How much time in your day is spent aimlessly on social media or surfing the net? Reclaim your time and invest it in ways to create more of what you want to experience.

Proclaim your focus on self-care. One of the most important beginning steps for focusing on self-care in your life is to make an internal commitment to yourself about the importance of doing this work now and continuing to live this way going forward. Internalize that this is your new way of life, period. Then, to seal the deal, proclaim it to other people in your life as well, including your immediate family, extended family, close friends, etc. There is tremendous power in sharing with others what you intend to do and taking a stand for yourself. It acts as an additional fire of motivation to stay committed. Share it any way you'd like—make a call, talk about it over a meal, or post it on your favorite social media outlets. Stake your claim.

The power of structured planning. While I will always passionately promote the idea of remaining flexible with expectations and outcomes and avoiding the urge to hold yourself to some idealistic self-care standard of living, I fundamentally believe that setting up some form of structure is nurturing. Having structure doesn't mean powering through self-care tasks, perhaps hating every second of them, just to achieve a certain desired healthy outcome. I do not promote getting stuck in the "should" mentality, which is highly demotivating and leads to unnecessary stress and anxiety. Having structure means honoring your intentions with an arrangement and framework that promotes the likelihood to experience what you want to experience, making powerful choices to start and be able to adjust as needed.

It's helpful to view your ideal way of living in self-care as an entity unto itself, where structure provides the foundation for your intentions and goals. The idea is to begin with your top priority self-care needs right now, set intentions and goals, then make a plan and go for it. Update your structure to meet your ever-evolving needs. Let it grow with you and support you all along the way. This also releases needless emotional turmoil around constantly trying to figure out how to manage self-care.

HOW TO CREATE YOUR SELF-CARE RHYTHM/FLOW:

As you've read through this book you've most likely noted the self-care areas that are your primary starting points. Based on your intentions and goals from the last two chapters, what action steps can you begin to take towards each goal that support that goal and your self-care needs and also make you feel alive in your life? You can only make decisions on what you know right now. So, start there.

The next step is to commit to one to three of these action steps for the next two weeks. Only one to three new action steps in total, out of all of the goals you might have recorded. The super-secret is that in order to make it real, schedule those activities on your calendar, like an appointment. Schedule reminders for each activity so that you get a poke to remember to take care of yourself in whatever ways you've identified. View this time for yourself as a meeting with the most important person you know.

The basic flow is to try on new action steps to address your intentions and goals every two weeks. Before you select new ones, determine how things are going with the current action steps and see what you might need to shift. Do a small evaluation before you add any new steps to your life. Drop the ones you've tried that aren't serving you. As the weeks and months progress, continue to adjust, adding and subtracting self-care action steps to best meet your self-care needs and success. Doing this creates your particular rhythm and flow. As you practice more self-care you can adjust your plan to honor your expanded awareness.

ᵉ SELF-CARE DARE ᵉ
YOUR INSPIRED ACTION STEPS

Look back on your goal worksheet and assign one to two inspired action steps per goal that you will dive into in the next two weeks. Then, schedule them on your calendar. Do this same process every two weeks.

CHAPTER TWENTY-FIVE

«— SUPPORT AND ACCOUNTABILITY —»

In my experience, the two biggest missing ingredients for follow-through on new endeavors, especially those related to self-care, are support and accountability. They really are the super-secret ingredients to living a juicy, meaningful life filled with daily self-care rituals. It is our fundamental human nature to be seen and heard and to feel like someone cares enough to hold us to a bigger version of ourselves. I heard a song recently that said that we need someone to hear us when we sigh. Yes, that's totally it. While we are ultimately responsible for our own outcomes, there is a momentum that gets created with proper support and accountability, which simply does not exist otherwise. As you support yourself in this journey, you actually open the door to receiving support from the world around you. The other super-secret is to open your heart so that you can prepare to graciously receive that support as well.

WAYS TO BUILD YOUR SUPPORT SYSTEM AND FURTHER CONSTRUCT TEAM YOU

Identify and resolve any missing links in your support system—ones that will actually allow you to focus time and energy on self-care habits and mastermind ways to fill those gaps. Here are some scenarios to consider:

- ☑ If need be, have courageous (honest, meaningful, purposeful, direct) conversations with those who mean the most to you. Identify who you most need support from and tell them what you want them to know. Say what you need to say, ask what you need to ask, and invite them into a conversation about what you really need, while also being mindful of anything that comes up around what they need as well. It is no coincidence that the people who move mountains in their lives are genius at these conversations. Think of those conversations you have had in your life that have made all the difference. Those words shared with someone who matters most to you in your life are most likely partly responsible for who you are right now today. Transformation can come from a single conversation.

- ☑ Come right out and ask for any emotional support you need. Who can support you best? Identify the specific ways they can help, then be fearless and ask. Perhaps you can even create a sort of "power support partnership" with another friend and support her in a particular endeavor as well. Check in regularly with each other to stay accountable. I personally have many of these relationships to support my efforts on particular projects, and they are my lifeline.

✓   Hang up your supermom cape. Moms, married or single, I give you permission to hang up your supermom cape and empower your kids with more responsibility, if need be, to help free up some time for you to focus on your self-care needs. Also, if you have family or friends that can help with childcare, ask them and let them help. If you don't have a natural, built-in childcare system, hire a nanny or babysitter. Do not let the lack of childcare be an excuse for not taking care of yourself and doing the things that truly nourish you. If you don't already know of a responsible person you can hire, look to other resources like <u>care.com</u>.

✓   If you live with other people, empower them with more responsibility. You do not have to do it all. In what ways can your roommates or family be more supportive? How about meal planning, grocery shopping, food preparation, kitchen help, cleanup, laundry, housecleaning, yardwork, or other household chores? Rethink and redistribute responsibilities and create more time in your life to focus on desired activities. If you don't live with anyone and have the means to do so, hire out as much of this work as you can.

ᵜ Stay inspired. Who positively influences you? Spend
more time with people who raise your game and
hold you to a bigger version of yourself. We represent
the average of the five people we hang out with the
most. Who are you hanging out with? Is it time
to reach out for some new energy in your life?

ᵜ Honor your boundaries. Remember how we talked about
setting healthy and sacred boundaries for yourself? It
seems important to mention that concept again here,
because it is absolutely part of your support system to
stay conscious of the boundaries you need in order to
focus on self-care. This is where you really get to take
a stand for yourself and learn to say no to others so
you can say yes to yourself and learn that it's okay to
let people down if necessary. You absolutely cannot
be responsible for the way everyone feels. You can
be respectful of their feelings, but not responsible.

When I was pulling myself out of my desperate, depressive
funk, one of the things I desired most was more support. My husband
was the only person I really depended on in that way at that time, and
he was living and working, and still does live and work, in another
state most of the time. I spent a lot of time feeling sorry for myself
and using my circumstances as an excuse for why I couldn't attend
events, go out with friends, participate in physical activity, and more.
As you may recall from the beginning of the book, I was running
my business, managing the family finances and almost all aspects of

the household. I was single-parenting during the week, coping with some serious physical conditions, dealing with issues regarding my grandmother, and essentially losing my mind trying to be present and effective in all of these roles. On top of that, I was an epic perfectionist to boot. It was totally depleting me. Instead of being continuously disappointed by the ways people *weren't* showing up for me, I knew I had to build my own support system. Over the years, I've put many things into practice, but I thought I'd share a couple of the most impactful ones:

  ☑   I set up a carpool to help with driving kids to school in the mornings and taught my kids how to perform all of the necessary steps to get ready in the mornings on their own. For me, the best time of day to get some structured movement in is first thing in the morning, right after I wake up and finish meditation. But I was feeling chained to the house, because I had to help the kids get ready in the mornings and drive them to school. I could have probably gotten up even earlier to go to the gym, but the idea of a four-in-the-morning gym date was not nourishing in any way. By setting up the carpool and teaching my kids how to use an alarm, prepare easy breakfast meals, and responsibly prepare for their days, I was able to buy myself the opportunity to get some physical activity in during my optimal hours on the weeks when I wasn't driving the carpool myself. This was a huge win for me. Yes, it took a several weeks for the kids and me to get into a new routine, but to this day, it has been so worth it. An added bonus was that they began to feel empowered by their ability to navigate the kitchen themselves. They continue to explore in the kitchen in other ways as well, like preparing other easy recipes and cleaning up after themselves, which is extra awesome bonus.

∨ I am a chef. I enjoy cooking, but that doesn't mean that I enjoy everything related to what it takes to put a meal on the table. It's no small feat to be responsible for meal planning, grocery shopping, unloading groceries, prepping for and cooking the meal, setting the table, and cleaning up. And then, after going through all of the prep, service, and cleanup, if anyone even looked at me wrong or hinted at the possibility that they were not enjoying what I had prepared, I wanted to throw my hands up and say, "Forget it. I'm not cooking for you people anymore." Being the household cook can be a thankless task. But because I have certain philosophies about how I'd like to feed myself and my family most of the time, it isn't really an option not to prepare healthy, home-cooked meals. It was another one of the areas I addressed in building my support system. I called a family meeting to talk about how I was feeling regarding my overwhelm with being responsible for all aspects of getting healthy meals on the table. We talked about ways to split up the process. We considered who could take responsibilities for the different steps. I still do most of the cooking, but I no longer do many of the other parts of the process, and life is so much better as a result. Resentment was removed and energetic space was created for more self-care.

౿ SELF-CARE DARE ౿
YOUR EXTRA SUPPORT

What extra support do you need to be able to truly focus on your self-care goals? What steps can you take to get that support?

CHAPTER TWENTY-SIX

«— DISMOUNTING INTO YOUR DAY —»

How you start (and end) each and every day can have a massive impact on your life. It's like the bookends of your day and it can greatly impact what happens in between those time periods. I heard a speaker once share how he DISMOUNTS into his day, and this philosophy has stuck with me ever since. It provided a great visual, almost like vaulting off the side of my bed or down my stairs into an awesome day. In my vision, I'd stick the landing every time, of course.

The basic idea is that you create a set of habits, of things you do each morning that set you up for inevitable success. This sets the tone and mood for all your activities for the remainder of the day. It takes some thought to put together and will likely change as you transform, but it's a fun and powerful concept. For some, it might be waking up at a certain time each day, making and drinking a fresh vegetable juice, going for a thirty-minute walk, and sitting in silence for ten minutes before even looking at their schedule or phone. For others, it could be to not set an alarm, waking up naturally, dropping to the floor, and doing some yoga or light stretching, then having a cup of tea. It can be anything that serves you. It's your set of habits and practices that helps you get on track for the best day ever, each day, every day.

Here is how I do it. To have the best day ever, I like to be awake by 5:00 a.m., no matter what day of the week it is. I rarely sleep in. I like to be up before the sun and get going. When I first started this ritual, I had to set an alarm, but it's so ingrained now that my body's natural clock works like a charm. My internal clock is set, so I just naturally wake up. Then, before even getting out of bed, I stick my headphones in my ears, plug them into my smart phone, and play a guided meditation. Those usually last about twenty minutes. I generally take an additional twenty to thirty minutes in silence (not falling asleep again) or listening to a song from a meditation playlist I've created and simply list in my head and connect with the feelings of gratitude for everything in my life that I am deeply thankful for. I then get out of bed and get myself ready for whatever intentional movement I have scheduled for myself that morning, if I have it planned to do so. I usually plan on no more than an hour-and-a-half for my movement time, from the time I leave the house till the time I arrive back home. Before I leave the house, I prepare a tumbler of water to take with me for movement and drink a quick power shake of powdered greens and protein, then I'm out the door to *move*. When I arrive back home, I prepare and eat a balanced breakfast, shower, get dressed, grab a beverage (tea or flavored water), and begin my work day. Being self-employed, I've determined that my ideal workday begins at 9:00 a.m., so I complete this entire morning sequence to dismount into my day by that time. This is my habit and my routine. I find that if I follow it, my days begin in a powerful and awesome way. I feel like I own my time and have made myself a priority. Then, as I begin my workday, I am able to be more present in that space. Of course, this morning routine will shift over time as my self-care needs evolve.

✑ SELF-CARE DARE ✑
YOUR MORNING RITUALS

What morning rituals can you set up to dismount into your day? When will you begin to try those rituals?

part 6

<< — TAKING RESPONSIBILITY — >>

Possibility is born out of responsibility.
~ Shelley Hunter Hillesheim

CHAPTER TWENTY-SEVEN
«— ASSESSING YOUR JOURNEY —»

As with anything that you dedicate valuable time to and create plans, schedules, and energy around, it's important to make time to stop every now and then and take note of how things are *really* going. We are not likely to be on full autopilot mode with every aspect of our commitment to self-care because, like many self-development efforts, it's a continuous work in progress. And while some things will certainly become new habits, we still want to take time to connect with where we are, reflect on what's going well and what might need some attention, and make adjustments from there.

Even when you "know better" and are highly committed to living a life of regular, ongoing self-care, you can come to recognize that self-care is not happening. The most amazing, self-honoring connection happens when you are able to notice that it's not happening and then course-correct. That is only possible when you know fully where you are at any given moment.

It's important to regularly take assessment of your efforts, finding the areas where you are thriving and noting the areas of continued discomfort. Even though discomfort is an inevitable part of growth, it's still critical to take note of where those discomforts occur in our own lives. Struggles build our resilience muscles. There is nothing more graceful than the beauty of resilience.

You cannot know light unless you also know darkness. So, are you experiencing any discomforts and darkness in your self-care commitments? If so, where and in what way? Why do you think that is happening? Only from spending time on questions like these can you then make decisions about how to choose something different, giving you the awareness to move through the resistance and find your way back to the light, while still being in gratitude for the opportunities to see the darkness and grow from those experiences.

Tap into your courage, moment to moment, every single day. Stay committed to it and re-commit as often as necessary to stay on track. Always remember that you get to choose how this will go. If you don't feel empowered to choose, get still and re-connect to the fact that you actually do get to choose. In each moment, you are only one decision away from a totally different life. Take full responsibility for your life. If you take responsibility for everything in your life, then you have the opportunity to do anything. It's your CHOICE.

You have set up your healthy boundaries and you have created mindful self-care action steps that take your needs into consideration. You will work the plan to the best of your ability, but if you get too caught up in it having to be a certain way, you might set yourself up for disappointment. Rigidity can lead to serious stress and anxiety. There is beauty and grace in going with the flow and finding the lessons and magic in all situations. If it can't be exactly what you thought, ask yourself how you can make the best of it.

As a final reflection, take some time to review your journaled intentions and completed goal sheet for a moment. Then, consider the following questions:

- ✔ What barriers do you anticipate that might prevent you from achieving your self-care goals? What stories continue to show up as excuses and self-sabotage? Write them down in your self-care journal.
- ✔ For each item you've listed, write an idea next to it that could be an empowered way to overcome that barrier.
- ✔ Consider what you need to put in place for you to experience inevitable success. Look at both short-term and long-term ideas.

Yes, the path to self-care is a choice, but that choice can sometimes take courage on a minute-by-minute basis. Sometimes it requires that you re-commit and stand up for yourself—saying yes to you as often as necessary to honor your absolute, fundamental self-care needs. Sometimes it also requires that you tread carefully as you reflect back on how things have been going, while being conscious to stay out of the minefield of judgment.

It's okay to make new commitments as often as you need in order to stay consistent. It's incredibly rewarding to set up a plan and stick to it, but this work will absolutely require that you mind the gap between where you are currently and what you truly want to be like, live like, and feel like. As we've previously looked at, this is not meant to be a rigid set of principles that you must adhere to or else. It's a very gentle and fluid process.

FEEDBACK (NOT SETBACKS)

When we take the time to reflect on our actions and progress from any given starting point, being able to forgive what we weren't able to accomplish is a fundamental factor in anyone's progressive journey, and it's actually an art form in and of itself. This is not a time to beat ourselves up about what we didn't do. It is, however, a time to take note of what actions we can celebrate and what we may want to spend more time nurturing as we go forward.

It's all feedback. One of the most powerful mindset shifts in the area of self-assessment is being able to perceive all things, not only on this self-care journey, but in life, as feedback rather than setbacks. It's all there to help us learn about our edges and to see where we can grow and expand. It's critical to release the idea that the past could have been any different. It's essential that you be able to let go of the past you thought you wanted. Letting go is another *choice* available to us.

View opportunities for improvement as areas that still need work and identify what might be more optimal going forward until you reach your ideal outcome. Always remain flexible in your thinking and absolutely, positively, love yourself through the process. It can be extremely helpful when faced with decisions about how to make more empowering choices around self-care to ask yourself this question: "If I truly loved myself, what would I do next to get back into a more empowered stance with my self-care practices?" Go with whatever comes to your mind first and don't judge it.

The only thing we are called to do is the next right thing, so when you feel lost, confused, or overwhelmed, all you really need to do is the next right thing for you. I am certain that when you go within you'll know what that next right thing is. You already do. If you don't think you do, then get still long enough to connect with your inner guide to hear it. Slow down, get honest with yourself, and listen. Cultivate the ability to step in between the stimulus of a circumstance and your response to it. Everything is a choice, even choosing NOT to do what might feel like the next right thing.

When you find yourself off track, internally acknowledge that you aren't where you want to be and make a conscious commitment to get back on track. Re-connect with your version of what's best for you, being fully aware that your best can change from day to day, hour to hour, month to month, and year to year. Be conscious enough to flip on the light switch to see what may be going on. One of the surest signs of wholeness—physical, emotional, and mental—is how fast you can bounce back. Sometimes we need to process. Take that time. Accept the messages, take notes, determine what purpose that moment of discomfort is serving and then release it. Then, escort any disempowering thoughts out of your mind. Meditation and movement are two great ways to do that.

Connect with your inner wisdom *more consistently*. Quite honestly, that is one of the most fundamental reasons why I do what I do—to help myself and others achieve this connection. The idea is to identify, get motivated, and sustain enthusiasm for your goals instead of getting all fired up and then losing your momentum the very next day. Being able to check in with yourself to get clarity and then being willing to get real about what you need now is part of the critical mindset work that helps build up your self-care foundation and will be a secret weapon that helps you stay committed to nourishing and flourishing Team YOU.

If you are still struggling, bring in your self-care reinforcements by connecting to the support system you learned about (and hopefully established) as you made your way through the book.

CELEBRATING SUCCESSES AND START A WHAT'S GOING WELL JOURNAL

Celebrate your self-care successes, even in the smallest ways, regularly. Make it part of your habits. If you already have a gratitude journal, add a small section for celebrations of your specific self-care action items. Or start a separate little notebook where you record daily what's going well with your new self-care habits. Call it a "What's Going Well Journal." This trains you to see what's going right in your life, which is actually scientifically proven to increase happiness, clarity, and vitality (according to Robert Emmons' research in his book called *Thanks*).

Being in gratitude and being able to celebrate all of the steps you are taking to nourish and flourish your self-care needs is an ultimate secret ingredient to continuous forward momentum. And, as an added bonus, counting your blessings instead of sheep is like a secret sleeping pill. Grateful people sleep better, which creates optimal health. I encourage you to be in "grateful flow" all day long. Stop and take note any time you feel gratitude for being able to nurture yourself and sit with it for a moment before moving on. Even something as seemingly insignificant as a hot shower is a reason to be thankful. Just think of all that had to happen and how many people/ organizations were involved in making it possible for you to have a hot shower. Continuously connect with being grateful and use the feeling of peace as your inner compass, as your center. When you're able to do that, you know you've nailed it with your self-care habits. Not perfection, but contentment with your journey and the habits you've committed to in order to honor yourself consistently.

WEEKLY SELF-REVIEW

One very tangible activity you can do to check in with yourself is to spend fifteen to twenty minutes each week doing a more formal review of what you said you wanted to accomplish and comparing it to what you did accomplish to meet your self-care needs. Don't go overboard. Just write a small summary in your self-care journal to note what's going well (to celebrate) and then what you will change in the coming week. I recommend doing this on Sunday night each week and encourage you to take notes throughout the week to incorporate into your self-review. It's also nourishing to read this information at some later date, as you grow into new habits and reflect on the changes.

COACHING

None of the ideas, principles, and practices outlined in this book are difficult. But I do know that it takes focus and sacred discipline to truly live with self-care at the core of your life. If any of this feels too overwhelming, yet you *know* instinctively that you need to focus more on self-care in your life, you may want to consider hiring a coach to help. A great coach who is dedicated to whole-person health, lifestyle, and self-care can help you bridge the gap from where you are now to where you want to be. They can serve as expert guides to help you get outside of yourself and your stories and provide the support and accountability necessary for you to transform how you are living at a much faster pace than you might be able to do on your own. An excellent coach can also provide you with an incredible gift that we don't often get in our lives—the gift of presence.

I have used, and still use, a variety of coaches to help me with my own life and business. They have become my support and accountability gurus and a big part of Team ME, helping me sort out the muck, get clear, and stay in inspired motion. It has been an indispensable tool in my life.

As a self-care coach, one of the most profound gifts I offer to my clients is the gift of presence, which I believe is the greatest gift you can give another human being. I am able to sit with and hear my clients, really listening to what they have to say. I am honored to see them, hear them, and hold space for them, not only providing guidance, but allowing them to sit in their own power and hear themselves talk. Magic happens in that space. In my role as a coach, I understand that I am an agent for change, offering a life-transforming, sacred contract with my clients. I like to think of it as a roadmap to serenity where I can help illuminate their journey. While I always practice the art of honoring the core of each client's being, I also provide, without force, a dose of reality along with loving encouragement.

Working with a coach of any kind need not be a lifelong commit, but it is often a great place to set the fire under your

behind when and if you need it. You can work with someone as
long as necessary in order to get you to where you want to go in a
meaningful, thoughtful, and consistent way.

∽ SELF-CARE DARE ∽
BEGINNING YOUR ASSESSMENT

What did you most connect with in this chapter as ways
to assess your journey? How will you handle them? When will
you begin? In what ways could you use the support of a coach?
What kind of coach would you want to work with? Take action
on beginning the research necessary to find someone who will
best suit your needs.

CHAPTER TWENTY-EIGHT
←— YOUR SELF-CARE VISION BOARD CREDO —→

‿ THE FINAL DARE... ‿
LIVE LIKE YOU MEAN IT...

Your self-care journey is a personal one. Only you truly know what you need and how to nourish your body, mind, and soul. I sincerely hope that reading this book has given you some awareness about the importance of making yourself a priority and the steps you can take to begin that powerful journey of constructing a robust Team YOU.

As our final, and perhaps most important, Self-Care Dare, you will develop your very own Self-Care Vision Board Credo. A credo is a set of fundamental beliefs and guiding principles. It integrates your intentions with inspired actions that bring purpose, meaning, and significance to your life. This will help inspire your commitment and stand as a reminder when you need a swift kick of motivation. The intent is to make it as bold, beautiful, and courageous as you can. Once it's created, post it somewhere visible so you can see it regularly. Look at it daily and read out loud to yourself any words you've included. For an extra dose of accountability, share it with others on Team YOU, so your support team knows what you are up to and can gently and lovingly point to it if you should waver in your commitment to yourself and your self-care needs.

This credo will declare your core values and beliefs around self-care, what you stand for, and how you intend to honor yourself in this space. It's a compass pointing you toward what you've decided is your true north in this process. It's also a mechanism for focusing your mind and reminding you of your priorities. It is a source of motivation and a behavior modification reminder so you always act in accordance with your values, even during times of stress. Ultimately, it's a gentle reminder about how you intend to live and bring awareness into your new way of living, each and every day.

Let this credo be a guiding light for you and a way to focus your energies on this work. Ultimately, self-care is giving yourself every opportunity to live by your values and principles to achieve what is most important to you. Your credo is your proclamation to honor yourself, always. It's self-care credo time! Here's how to do it.

GUIDELINES FOR CREATING YOUR PERSONAL CREDO

Refer to the sample credo to get a visual representation of our end goal with this powerful exercise. You can view and download it at *www.selfcare101book.com/bonus*. Then, prepare to create your own credo. It can take as little as an hour to complete. However, don't limit yourself. Spend whatever time you need. Make space in your calendar to craft this. It solidifies your self-care commitment in a profound and meaningful way.

Compile Your Building Blocks. You can create a *hard copy* or *digital* version of your credo. The choice is yours. The basic construction elements are the same. If you choose to go digital, consider using a program like *Canva.com* to put your project together. There are many online tutorials to help.

What you're creating is a one-page credo that you can update anytime you wish. I encourage you to update it as often as necessary to keep it fresh and motivating, every three months perhaps. At the very least, I recommend that you change it up twice per year.

Step 1: Find a single image of you (just you) that you will use for this project. I recommend selecting a picture that represents the most authentic you, an image that makes you smile from the inside out when you look at it.

- Hard copy – print a copy of the picture.
- Digital – note the image name and where it is saved on your computer so you can access it and move it into your digital project when you are ready.

Step 2: Review your journal notes and any work on the Self-Care Dares and exercises you completed. Then, make a list of the self-care practices that you want to address first—your highest priority action steps. Here are the mind, body, and soul self-care principles we covered:

BODY

- ✔ Loving your body
- ✔ Addressing nagging ailments
- ✔ Nourishment
- ✔ Movement
- ✔ Play
- ✔ Sleep

MIND AND SOUL

- ✔ Downtime
- ✔ Silence/Stillness/Meditation
- ✔ Gratitude
- ✔ Community and Connection
- ✔ Self-Expression and Service

Step 3: Review what you wrote in your self-care journal about how you want your life to be. With self-care as your priority, what do you want your life to look like and feel like? What do you want to experience differently and what are you willing to do to achieve it? How do you want to live on a daily basis? Here are the concepts regarding mindset and setting yourself up for success that might be helpful to review as you do this step. Are there any concepts related to mindset that resonate with you more than others? Note all of your thoughts.

HONORING YOU

- ✔ Courageous Inquiry
- ✔ The Power of CHOICE

✓ Setting Healthy Boundaries

✓ Clearing the Clutter

✓ The Power of Planning

SETTING UP FOR INEVITABLE SUCCESS

✓ Setting intentions

✓ Moving from intentions to goals

✓ Releasing the "busy" mindset

✓ Setting up support and accountability

✓ Preparing for the best day ever

Step 4: Review everything you've noted in preparing for this project so far. Spend time reflecting on what you wrote and how it makes you feel. Then, write a list (in no particular order) of words, statements, images, and/or quotes that summarize how you intend to make and keep self-care a priority in your life; everything that will support you and remind you of your self-care mission. Do Internet searches to help. Search mottos, picture quotes, etc., and find inspirations that encapsulate the way you want to feel about your self-care journey.

✓ Hard copy – cut out what you wrote down as quotes, sayings, etc., or print hard copies of quotable images or words that you found on the Internet.

✓ Digital - copy and save images to a folder on your computer to paste into your virtual credo

✓ Additionally, online design software programs will let you create fun and fancy words, phrases with outlines, colors, etc. Tap into your creativity.

TIPS – To create personal messages, use powerful, present-tense language. Use I statements, such as "I am {fill in the blank}", "I {add whatever verb makes sense}", etc. This is the time to stand in your truth. Connect with your inner wisdom and take note of what it wants you to know.

Assemble Your One-Page Credo. Select a patterned or colorful background to use, either on paper or virtually from a software program. Place the image of yourself somewhere on the sheet first. You may end up moving it around, but you have to start somewhere.

Start placing phrases, words, quotes, and other images around the page. Do not be particular about this. Embrace your innate creativity and place them randomly. Make each of them look different—a different font, color, size, with a circle around some, squares around others, maybe a heart, too. Move things around until you achieve what feels like a totally inspiring CREDO and then call it done.

Post it where you can refer to it often. You may be motivated to post it online or somewhere where others can read it. If you feel so inspired, post it to your social media page using #selfcare101book. This can provide an extra dose of accountability for you!

Here's a sample of the statements I collected for my own life from Step 4 to provide you with a dose of inspiration. Following the format described above, these statements were derived based on reviewing my intentions, goals, action steps, and everything I want to do in my life to honor my self-care needs. The credo that you will see online is built from these statements.

1. I am the #1 priority in my life. It has to start here.

My needs come first. I focus on my self-care needs every day so that I am putting my oxygen mask on first, always. This is not selfish, and I release all guilt that might make me feel like it is selfish. I give from the overflow. My most pressing self-care needs at this moment are daily meditation, regular movement, and high quality nutrition. I treat my body, mind, and soul with respect. This is my way of life.

2. I make space for PLAY often.

Play, play, play is my new mantra! I regularly look for opportunities to engage in activities that feel like play. I do not make this something that I schedule; instead, I look for present-moment opportunities and take them as often as I can. I determine what means "fun" to me.

3. I accept me, as is, at all times, and I do not allow myself to shrink for others or be influenced by what they might think of me.

I graciously accept the opinions of others but do not allow those opinions to influence me. I stand firm in my power and my beliefs about who I am and what I need. I cannot please everyone and that's totally okay.

4. I surround myself with people who make me want to be a better version of myself.

My most intimate circle of influence is comprised of the people I spend the most time with. I choose who that is, and I honor myself by spending time with people and in circumstances that help me honor my authentic superpowers and sparkle. When I spend time with them, I am uplifted and inspired.

5. I set healthy boundaries and release toxicity from my life.

The people and circumstances in my life that are draining me need to be released. I no longer allow anything to sap my powerful energy or commitment to self-care. It's not personal; it's my right. I own it, have courageous conversations, and take action as needed.

6. I spend time in gratitude and grace each and every day.

This is the most powerful way to stay present, connect with my worthiness, and stay in appreciation of others. Period. I share my gratitude with others regularly, so they know they are appreciated.

7. I stay in alignment with my passion and what I stand for every single day.

If I feel out of alignment, the minute I am aware, I hit the reset button and find my way back to center.

8. I welcome fear and discontentment, but I do not allow them to consume me.

If I feel fear or discontentment, I acknowledge what I am feeling and sit with it to see if there is any wisdom in it, but I always recognize that I did not come here to play small. I quickly release fear and step back into my power.

9. I live my passion and purpose and I share my light with the world.

I not only practice what I teach, I embody it, and I am an inspiring example to other women of how they can do it for themselves. This is my way of giving back the gifts that have been given to me. I do work that is meaningful and deeply connected with my passion and purpose.

After writing these statements, I did an Internet search for images, words, quotes, and phrases that reflect them. Those inspired images, single words, or phrases are what goes on the one-page Self-Care Credo.

❧ SELF-CARE DARE ❧
YOUR SELF-CARE CREDO

Hop online and review the Self-Care Credo I prepared as a sample. You can view and download it at
www.selfcare101book.com/bonus
Now, follow the steps outlined in this chapter and complete your own. If you would like to share it, please do so by using #selfcare101book.

← CONCLUSION →

I may not know you personally, but I believe in you. Even on the days when you don't believe in yourself. I am 100% confident that you are capable of doing anything you set your mind to do. It's an undeniable fact of our human existence. You choose. You control your destiny, with self-care or anything else. I can guarantee you that focusing on meeting your self-care needs is a game-changer.

Everything I've shared and provided in *Self-Care 101* will help you navigate your way to nourishing and flourishing Team YOU. This is the place where you've bridged the gap between knowing who you can be and who you actually are. That beautiful space is where you align with your true self. You find it by taking actions every day in a loving, self-nurturing way to honor yourself. There is a crucial connection that happens when you care for yourself in a loving way.

It is the self-care *sweet spot*. My deepest hope is that you can use the tools in this book to find that for yourself. And when you do, cherish it with your entire being. You deserve it. It's time to come alive and to bring some more "life" into your life.

Remember to be kind and to love yourself through this process. It took a lifetime to get where you are. It will take more than a minute to get into the groove of new habits that support you differently. Feel them out, try them on, and make continuous adjustments. It's always a work in process and it can be a beautiful journey. It means you are growing, learning, and changing. I like to call it growing with the flow.

There are no rules. This is YOUR STORY, and you *get* to choose how it goes. If you are in need of a new beginning so you can live a life steeped in nourishing self-care habits, make the choice to begin right now. Then, begin again as often as you need. The only thing that matters is this moment, right now. It's your turn to uncover your beautiful truth. What's non-negotiable to you? Connect with that and create your powerful self-care boundaries around it. Protect it with your life by living your new habits.

Write your own script. Don't be stuck in a script that doesn't empower you. You are only one decision away from a totally different life. The bottom line is that no one else can prioritize your self-care needs but you. Give yourself permission and go. It's your purest and most vital form of fuel in this life.

Make a commitment to live on purpose. Make a commitment to live a life uncommon. Show up and do the work with intention. This is YOUR journey to a lifetime of self-care. Own it.

ACKNOWLEDGMENTS

As I longed to share my work in a bigger way and learned
to become a writer, I repeatedly heard the analogy that writing,
publishing, marketing, and continuing to nurture the book material
is much like childbirth and then child rearing. Having birthed two
children of my own and having spent the last twelve years of my life
as a parent, I would say from what I've experienced in this process
so far that this analogy is just about right. Just like raising a child, it
takes a village. With that in mind, I have certainly had a village of
amazing people to help me bring this project to life.

I am grateful beyond measure for the people who make up
Team ME and who have had such a significant impact on the journey
to learn to write and publish this book. While I am aware that I could
literally thank everyone I've come into contact with in my entire life,
because I know that all of those encounters and experiences led to this
moment, I want to shout out special love to those who had a direct
influence on my journey to make this book a reality.

To my husband and children – my deepest gratitude for your
unwavering support of all of my big ideas. Your love, support, and
encouragement have been the miracle I needed to stay in the game.
May I be an extra bright light to you all for living your dreams every
single day.

To my growing tribe – thank you for your encouragement
and support as I continue to navigate my way through my personal
growth journey and bring forth more new material to share. I don't
get to do this work if you don't exist.

I am blessed with a dedicated group of brilliant women who I
see as my intentionally cultivated dream team. Thank you to Donna

Mazzitelli (editor and angel) and Polly Leftosky for your enthusiasm and wisdom. You both helped me make this a much better book. A big thanks also to Stacey Lane for your tremendous creative contributions. To my coaches, mentors and way-showers, thank you for your expert guidance and for encouraging me to move through obstacles with grace, reset when needed and celebrate each milestone. I am incredibly grateful for how you hold me accountable to honoring my intensity, which is the ultimate fuel behind the passion for the work that is mine to do in this world.

Thank you to the Integrative Institute of Nutrition for offering the coaching program I attended and for the book writing program. I greatly appreciated the nudge to even consider the possibility of writing and publishing a book.

I am absolutely blessed to be surrounded by a circle of remarkable women—my soul sisters—in supporting one another in light, laughter, and tears through all of life's experiences. I am very lucky to have many to thank, but I'd like to send special gratitude to my closest confidants, my mastermind group of women, my Real Life Book Club sisters, my spiritual "miracle mafi" bunch (you know who you are), neighbors and friends who are like family, and my social media family who continue to support and encourage my continued expansion.

Thank you to Deepak and Oprah for your powerfully crafted guided meditations to keep my mind sane through the creative process.

I'd also like to thank the multitudes of people, circumstances, and experiences that have each led me to be exactly who I am in this moment. My deepest gratitude for the profound effect on my life and, ultimately, my perspectives.

The best way to learn Shelley's techniques is to hear it straight from her

Photo credit: Britt Nemeth Photography

Shelley Hunter Hillesheim is an inspirational speaker, workshop leader, coach and transformational self-care maverick for ambitious, driven women. She is also extremely passionate about cultivating sisterhood among women to create a much-needed support system to play bigger in life.

As the founder of the comprehensive wellness coaching company, A Nourished Life, she rescues depleted high achievers from overwhelm and helps them create the spaciousness and simplicity needed in order to nourish themselves with sustainable self-care habits. This allows them to nurture their ambition without the continuous cycle of depletion and resuscitation.

Through Shelley's speaking, coaching, transformational group experiences, workshops and one-of-a-kind retreats, women learn how to integrate self-care practices into their daily rituals creating self-loving habits that change their mindsets and their lives.

Contact Shelley to release overwhelm and step into a new self-care journey.

www.ANourishedLife.net
www.SelfCare101Book.com